Mennonite Peace Theology

Mennonite Peace Theology

A Panorama of Types

Second Edition

Edited by John Richard Burkholder
and Barbara Nelson Gingerich

INSTITUTE OF MENNONITE STUDIES

Copyright © 2024 by Mennonite Central Committee

Published by Institute of Mennonite Studies
Anabaptist Mennonite Biblical Seminary
3003 Benham Avenue, Elkhart, IN 46517

First edition published 1991
Mennonite Central Committee Peace Office
Akron, PA

Library of Congress Cataloging-in-Publication Data

Names: Burkholder, John Richard, 1928-2019 editor. | Gingerich, Barbara Nelson, editor. | Mennonite Central Committee. | Institute of Mennonite Studies (Elkhart, Ind.)
Title: Mennonite peace theology : a panorama of types / edited by John Richard Burkholder and Barbara Nelson Gingerich.
Description: Second edition. | Elkhart, IN : Institute of Mennonite Studies, [2024] | Includes bibliographical references. | Summary: "Originally prepared for a 1989 joint session of the Mennonite Central Committee (MCC) Peace Committee and Ecumenical Peace Theology Work ing Group, the essays in this volume articulate and analyze ten distinct approaches to Mennonite peace theology: historic nonresistance, culturally engaged pacifism, social responsibility, apolitical nonresistance, the pacifism of the messianic community, radical pacifism, realist pacifism, Canadian pacifism, liberation pacifism, and neo-sectarian pacifism. This second addition adds an eleventh type: shalom political theology"— Provided by publisher.
Identifiers: LCCN 2024020011 | ISBN 9780936273600 (paperback)
Subjects: LCSH: Peace–Religious aspects–Mennonites. | Mennonites–Doctrines.
Classification: LCC BX8128.P4 M46 2024 | DDC 261.8/730882897–dc23/eng/20240514
LC record available at https://lccn.loc.gov/2024020011

International Standard Book Number: 978-0-936273-60-0 (paperback)

Cover design by Nathan Shumaker.

Cover image: Tomato plants thrive at a farm pilot project in Terituronné village, North Kanem, Chad, that Mennonite Central Committee supports through partner Association for the Promotion of Education (APE). An MCC team visited the farm in February 2024. Image credit: MCC photo/Wawa Chege.

In memory of J. R. Burkholder (1928–2019),
prophetic peacemaker

Contents

Foreword	ix
David C. Cramer	
Preface to the Second Edition	xi
Alain Epp Weaver	
Preface to the First Edition	xv
John A. Lapp	
Introduction	xvii
J. R. Burkholder and Barbara Nelson Gingerich	
Can We Make Sense of Mennonite Peace Theology?	1
J. R. Burkholder	

Ten Types of Mennonite Peace Theology

Type 1. Historic Nonresistance	11
J. R. Burkholder	
Type 2. Culturally Engaged Pacifism	19
Lauren Friesen	
Type 3. Social Responsibility	35
David Schroeder	
Type 4. Apolitical Nonresistance	41
J. R. Burkholder	

Type 5. The Pacifism of the Messianic Community   49
Helmut Harder

Type 6. Radical Pacifism   59
Barbara Nelson Gingerich

Type 7. Realist Pacifism   75
Lois Barrett

Type 8. A Perspective on Anabaptist Pacifism in Canada   87
John H. Redekop

Type 9. Liberation Pacifism   99
Robert Suderman

Type 10. An Emerging Neo-sectarian Pacifism   113
Daniel Schipani

Further Reflections

Reflections on Mennonite Uses of Anabaptist History   125
Arnold Snyder

Shalom Political Theology   129
A New Type of Mennonite Peace Theology for an Era of Discipleship
Malinda Elizabeth Berry

Afterword   153
Malinda Elizabeth Berry

Bibliography   155

Contributors   161

Foreword

Whenever I teach the course Christian Attitudes toward War, Peace, and Revolution at Anabaptist Mennonite Biblical Seminary (AMBS), I assign the booklet *Mennonite Peace Theology: A Panorama of Types*. The course offers a historical overview of Christian attitudes from the early church to the present, and *Mennonite Peace Theology* provides a helpful cross-section of Mennonite attitudes from the late 1980s and early 1990s in the United States and Canada. While the booklet has its quirks and is written by and for a prior generation, it continues to inspire students to imagine Mennonite peace theology not as a settled position but as an ongoing, lively conversation that they are invited to join.

I especially appreciate the way *Mennonite Peace Theology* decenters the approach of John Howard Yoder by placing it alongside nine other types. This decentering is crucial in light of the ongoing reckoning over Yoder's history of sexualized violence. Although Yoder's theology rose to prominence in Anabaptist and ecumenical spaces in the latter part of the twentieth century, this booklet demonstrates that there were always alternative perspectives. By doing so, it opens room for those who were shaped by Yoder's theology to engage with other perspectives, including those that explicitly address sexualized and gender-based violence as a problem for Mennonite peace theology.

Over the decades since its publication by Mennonite Central Committee (MCC) Peace Office in 1991, *Mennonite Peace Theology* has become unavailable to most readers outside of those who can access a copy through a Mennonite academic institution. Having witnessed first-hand how the booklet can inspire the imaginations of Anabaptist students, I am delighted that MCC has agreed to partner with the Institute of Mennonite Studies (IMS) at AMBS to publish this second edition.

This edition is newly designed and formatted. In-text citations have been moved to footnotes, and a bibliography has been added. Where a more recently version of a cited work is available, the updated information has been included in brackets. Otherwise, this edition maintains the integrity of the first, including the list of contributors, which reproduces the biographical information as it appeared in the 1991 edition.

In 2016, theologian Malinda Elizabeth Berry published an essay in *The Conrad Grebel Review* (CGR) that pays homage to the booklet by adding a new type of Mennonite peace theology: shalom political theology.

Her essay is included here as a new closing chapter to demonstrate how the original types can be creatively engaged to formulate new approaches to peace theology. IMS would like to thank the editors at *CGR* for their permission to republish Berry's essay.

IMS would also like to thank MCC for partnering on this project and the Schowalter Foundation for a generous grant that made this publication possible. This second edition is published in memory of J. R. Burkholder, who devoted his life and scholarship to prophetic peacemaking. Our hope is that this edition will enable a new generation of prophetic peacemakers to critically engage with voices who have come before in order to envision new ways of addressing violence in its many forms.

David C. Cramer
Managing Editor
Institute of Mennonite Studies
Elkhart, Indiana

Preface to the Second Edition

Alongside its practical relief, development, and peacebuilding work in the name of Christ, Mennonite Central Committee (MCC) has functioned over the course of more than a century as a catalyst for articulating shared Anabaptist understandings about peace theology, a space for inter-Anabaptist debates about the nature of the gospel of peace, and a mechanism for engaging broader ecumenical conversations about peace. *Mennonite Peace Theology: A Panorama of* Types—originally published by MCC in 1991 as a photocopied, 8 ½" x 11" booklet held together by a plastic spiral binder—stands as a significant milestone in this legacy of MCC support for and leadership of Anabaptist-Mennonite peace theology reflections.

This volume's subtitle promises to highlight a "panorama of types," pointing to the diverse, contested ways Anabaptists in Canada and the United States in the late 1980s and early 1990s understood the relationship between "theology" and "peace." That theological diversity has been with MCC since its inception in 1920 in the aftermath of the "war to end all wars" (even as war had clearly not come to an end, with MCC created to respond to the needs of fellow Mennonites in southern Russia living amid war and famine).

Both in its beginnings and in subsequent decades, MCC functioned as an expression of practical, inter-Anabaptist action—to feed the hungry in what became the Soviet Union, to assist Mennonite refugees fleeing the Soviet Union to resettle in Paraguay, and to engage the US government to ensure that Anabaptist conscientious objectors to war could undertake an alternative to military service through MCC-administered Civilian Public Service (CPS) camps during the Second World War and through MCC's Pax program after the war. Yet alongside fostering this practical collaboration, MCC—through its Peace Section established in 1942—also helped during these years to nurture shared understandings across Anabaptist groups in the United States and Canada about what a "peace theology" could look like. During the war, MCC published a series of six booklets for use in CPS camps to promote a common understanding of Mennonite history and shared understandings of mission, service, and the relationship of the individual and the church to the state, with leading Mennonite scholars such as Harold S. Bender, Guy F. Hershberger, C. Henry Smith, Edmund G. Kaufman, and P. C. Hiebert penning the booklets. During and after the war, MCC also published multiple booklets aiming to bolster traditional Mennonite refusal of military service to accompany the Peace Section's draft counseling work, while addressing novel questions such as whether Christians could serve in noncombatant roles.

The MCC Peace Section's efforts to promote peace theology discernment went beyond practical questions of military conscription, with the Peace Section and its successors creating spaces for inter-Mennonite discernment about the peace witness demanded by Christian faith. Sometimes this discernment resulted in common statements about shared theological convictions for peace. So, for example, in 1950 the Peace Section convened an inter-Mennonite consultation in Winona Lake, Indiana, to discuss how to understand "nonresistance" in the post-war period, with the gathered representatives from various Mennonite and Brethren in Christ conferences issuing a "Declaration of Faith and Commitment." Four decades later, MCC in 1993 developed a statement outlining "A Commitment to Christ's Way of Peace," which MCC commended to the Anabaptist churches to which it was accountable, with some of those churches adopting the statement as their own.

Also during the 1950s, the MCC Peace Section engaged broader ecumenical discussions about peace theology, giving leadership to work of the Continuation Committee of the Historic Peace Churches to formulate and submit shared testimony to the World Council of Churches about peace being God's will. MCC continued to give Mennonite leadership to these historic peace church conversations around peace theology, most recently collaborating with the Quakers and the Church of the Brethren to organize and sponsor a series of conferences and subsequent book publications in the first decade of the twenty-first century to contribute to the World Council of Churches' Decade to Overcome Violence, with these conferences and books highlighting Anabaptist peace theology and witness across Africa, Asia, and Latin America.

While the Winona Lake statement of 1950 bore witness to the ability of diverse Mennonite groups in the United States and Canada to discover and articulate shared theological understandings of and commitments to peace, Anabaptist understandings of what constitutes "peace theology" have remained varied and at times conflictual. Over the past seven decades, MCC and broader Anabaptist understandings of peace theology's scope have expanded, moving beyond a singular focus on military conscription to asking what a commitment to Christ's way of peace has to say to racism, hunger crises, global systems of economic exploitation and inequality, and legacies of colonialism, patriarchy, and more. Publications like the MCC *Peace Office Newsletter* highlighted these diverse Mennonite perspectives on the implications for how peace theologies might understand evolving social and political realities. The 1991 book on *Mennonite Peace Theology* reprinted here represented an effort to take a step back from the diverse forms Mennonite peace witness had taken to reflect on the theological "types" embedded within and shaping that varied witness.

As John A. Lapp noted in his 1991 preface to *Mennonite Peace Theology*, this book lacks contributors from the global Anabaptist church—aside from an essay by Argentinian theologian Daniel S. Schipani and an essay on "liberation pacifism" that interacts with Latin American liberation theology. Over the thirty years since this book was first published, MCC has learned much—albeit often haltingly and incompletely—about how a fuller, richer Anabaptist peace theology requires hearing from a much broader range of voices than represented in these pages, recognizing that peace theology is not only rooted in Scripture and core theological convictions but is also shaped by and responsive to the experiences and histories of individuals and communities.

Mennonite Peace Theology necessarily stands as a limited exploration of the diverse types of Anabaptist theological reflection on the gospel of peace. Yet it has also proven capable of stimulating global conversations among Anabaptists from widely divergent contexts. May the reissuing of *Mennonite Peace Theology* therefore stand not as a definitive panoramic rendering of Anabaptist peace theology today but rather as a spur to more vigorous efforts to understand and to encourage global conversation and mutual discernment amid the diverse theological ways Anabaptists worldwide articulate their commitment to Christ's way of peace.

Alain Epp Weaver
Director of Planning and Learning
Mennonite Central Committee
Akron, Pennsylvania

Preface to the First Edition

Once upon a time Mennonites were defined as a peace church. It was widely assumed, surely by most outsiders and probably many insiders, that Mennonite pacifism was rooted in a corporate commitment to follow the teachings of Jesus Christ. Fundamentally this meant loving all people including the enemy, and a refusal to participate in war. The reality was never that simple. Some Mennonites never quite became so devout in their praxis. Others developed positions that called for gradations of theological understanding and societal interaction.

This document picks up the pieces of what is now a family of positions regarding peace, in order to analyze and critique. The process of differentiation has been going on throughout most of the twentieth century in North America. The differentiation includes theological nuance, ecclesiastical vision, and political awareness. It does raise the interesting question: With so much diversity, are we still a church committed to peace?

The studies here are excellent. But this is not the last word. The writers are largely North American. What do Mennonites on the other five continents have to add to this typology? There is some reference to the larger Christian milieu from which so much of our thinking grows, but this is indeed much richer and deeper than that discussed here. The new *A Declaration of Peace: In God's People the World's Renewal Has Begun* (Scottdale and Kitchener, 1990) reflects an ecumenical conversation not well represented in these studies. Since these types come out of a specific set of experiences, it is also critical to understand the social context of each type defined in this analysis. Saying all this is not to minimize an excellent and important piece. This will be a valuable resource for students, pastors, and anyone interested in this basic Mennonite paradigm.

John A. Lapp
Executive Secretary
Mennonite Central Committee
Akron, Pennsylvania
January 1991

Introduction

How this project began

The papers collected in this booklet were first prepared for the November 1989 joint session of two committees sponsored by Mennonite Central Committee (MCC), the Peace Committee and the Ecumenical Peace Theology Working Group.

Both these working groups had concluded that it would be useful to review the diverse types of peace theology currently promoted by various segments of the Mennonite and Brethren in Christ (BIC) constituency. So, early in 1989 the MCC Peace Office called a joint meeting of the two groups, with the theme announced as a "Review of Current Strains of Mennonite/BIC Peace Theology."

The purposes of this review included: (1) to describe the types of Mennonite peace thought and their theological assumptions, (2) to seek a consensus on a perspective that would be useful to MCC, and (3) to consider how to articulate our perspective in interchurch and ecumenical contexts.

At the request of the committees, J. R. Burkholder prepared a working paper, "Can We Make Sense out of Mennonite Peace Theology?" which introduced a provisional listing of ten distinct theological views represented in the current "Anabaptist" constituency.

The conveners of the joint meeting, Herman Bontrager and Marlin E. Miller, selected seven of the types and asked individual participants to prepare response papers for the November 2-4 gathering. To further specify the task, the conveners posed two questions: (1) *How does each type affect how Mennonites/BIC function in the public arena?* and (2) *Is our peace witness at risk?*

Toward a descriptive typology

The November 1989 sessions generated discussion of both the typological framework and the content of the views presented. The committees called for further work on this material and appointed the editorial team. Thus the papers were eventually rewritten and edited for publication in the present format, together with several more papers requested by the editors to complete the panorama of types.

The collection begins with an abbreviated version of J. R. Burkholder's working paper with its initial typology; this identifies the starting point for the other contributions. Subsequent chapters are arranged roughly chronologically, beginning with the oldest types and moving to the most recent. (This order differs from J. R.'s original one.) By agreement of writers and editors, names for some of the types have been changed in an effort to express more adequately the substance of those types.

Five of the chapters represent new material. Ronald Sider did a brief analysis of "'Apolitical' Nonresistance" at the November meeting but was unable to furnish a written essay for this publication; J. R. Burkholder has written that chapter instead. "Radical Pacifism" was not dealt with in November because the Ecumenical Peace Theology Working Group had devoted its June 1988 meeting to a discussion of Ron Sider's writings. Barbara Nelson Gingerich drew in part on that conversation for her analysis of the type.

Lauren Friesen, who participated in the November 1989 gathering, has written chapter 3, on the development over three generations of a distinctive Russian Mennonite or Bethel College (Kansas) type of "Culturally Engaged Pacifism." This welcome contribution links themes from types 5 and 9 of the original typology. Friesen made use of a section of Lois Barrett's original paper that dealt with this tradition; both Friesen and Barrett had discerned a gap in the initial typology at this point.

John H. Redekop responded generously to a request for a survey of Canadian pacifism, giving particular emphasis to the political involvements of Anabaptist-Mennonites on the Canadian scene. Another Canadian, Arnold Snyder, has offered his reflections on the uses of Anabaptist history and spirituality for Mennonite pacifism.

Barbara Nelson Gingerich has carried major responsibility for revising and editing the papers submitted. John R. Burkholder assisted in editorial work and supervised the project. John K. Stoner of the MCC Peace Office arranged for publication.

We thank the writers for their diligence, tolerance, and patience in this cooperative venture.

John R. Burkholder
Barbara Nelson Gingerich
Goshen, Indiana
November 1990

Can We Make Sense of Mennonite Peace Theology?

J. R. Burkholder

This chapter is a shortened version of the working paper prepared in 1989 for the November discussion. The assignment as I understood it was to provide some raw materials and tools for the task of describing Mennonite views on peace and church-state issues. So I hurriedly worked up a three-part background paper that was sent to the list of participants. The first section was called "Summarizing the twentieth century of Mennonite thought"; in it I brought together excerpts from some earlier writings, including several essays for the forthcoming *Mennonite Encyclopedia*, volume 5.[1] Some of that material is presented here in the chapter on "Historic Nonresistance."

In the second part of that preliminary document, I sketched a proposed typology of Mennonite peace theologies. I called this listing "provisional"; it was a first-draft brainstorm set forth simply as a device to provoke some thoughtful response. In a September mailing, Herman Bontrager and Marlin Miller adapted it as a framework for assigning papers to be prepared and discussed at the November meeting. Those papers, plus several more, appear now in this publication, some of them after significant reworking.

Although I am not particularly proud of that beginning typology, I am presenting the original outline here, only slightly edited, so that readers may understand the pattern around which this project began. (Revised names of some types appear in brackets after the original labels.) We are also including the third part of my earlier paper, "A working paradigm of basic issues," because some of the writers have used that analytical framework in organizing their essays.

A provisional typology of Mennonite peace theologies

There are several ways to develop a typology. One is primarily inductive: identify and select representative positions with some basic distinguishing

---

1 [Cornelius J. Dyck and Dennis D. Martin, eds., *The Mennonite Encyclopedia*, vol. 5 (Scottdale, PA: Herald Press, 1990). See also John R. Burkholder, "Nonresistance," *Global Anabaptist Mennonite Encyclopedia Online*, gameo.org.]

features (either schools of thought or major figures) and then set forth the major elements of each view. This is the approach of H. Richard Niebuhr's *Christ and Culture* (1951), of John H. Yoder's *Nevertheless* (1971), and of Duane Friesen's MCC booklet (1982).[2] It has the advantages of relative faithfulness to the intentions of the authors and groups and of being more narrative and expository in form, but it may lack in specificity and clarity of comparison.

Another approach is more deductive and analytical: determine some of the key variables that are important to the discussion, organize these elements into a rational structure of some sort, and use this as a grid for examining the various viewpoints. This is a more rigorous method but tends to squeeze the life out of the subjects and may lead to forced categorization.

In the initial discussions leading to the call for a paper of this kind, five or six positions held by representative Mennonites were identified. I was asked to prepare a conceptual map, presumably using an inductive model. On that basis, I have boldly sketched some representative positions, identifying them using my own labels, and noted the names of some obvious proponents, along with some distinctive characteristics.

Following that is an analytical grid intended as a framework for the necessary further work of sorting out the method and meaning of these respective views. In other words, I am offering some raw material that reflects both the inductive and deductive approaches.

It must be emphasized that this listing is limited to the contemporary Mennonite/BIC scene. As over against the manifold varieties of peace positions in Yoder's *Nevertheless* (to say nothing of other more warlike ethical and political stances), these views all hold much in common: (1) they all claim to be standing within the Anabaptist tradition, (2) all reject lethal violence as an option for Anabaptist believers, (3) all claim the authority of Scripture, and (4) all would posit the church community as a primary loyalty.

---

2 H. Richard Niebuhr, *Christ and Culture* (New York: Harper & Row, 1951); John H. Yoder, *Nevertheless: The Varieties of Religious Pacifism* (Scottdale, PA: Herald Press, 1971 [2nd ed., 1992]; Duane Friesen, *Mennonite Witness on Peace and Social Concerns: 1900–1980* (Akron, PA: Mennonite Central Committee, 1982).

1. Historic Nonresistance

Proponents include Guy F. Hershberger, Harold S. Bender, and John C. Wenger. This is the baseline, especially for the (Old) Mennonite Church.

- This position stresses literal obedience to the teaching of Jesus in Matthew 5: resist not evil, turn the other cheek, love your enemies.
- It is expressed in conscientious objection to military service.
- It seeks alternatives to violence in other areas of life.
- It does not expect to reform the social order.

2. "Apolitical" Nonresistance

Proponents include Sanford Shetler, J. Ward Shank, James Hess, J. Otis Yoder, *Guidelines for Today*, and *The Sword and Trumpet*. (Although I question the appropriateness of the term, the "apolitical" label has been Shetler's recurring usage.")

- This position claims to be the legitimate offspring of "Historic Nonresistance" but holds a stringent two-kingdom view and seems to suggest that "what's wrong for us (killing) maybe right for them," although this interpretation has been denied by their spokespeople.
- It tends to favor traditional Old Testament political categories.
- It regards some forms of political activity as acceptable for individual Christians but not for the church as a body.

3. Radical Pacifism

Proponents include Dale Brown and Ron Sider.

- This type affiliates the rigorous nonviolent ethic of Jesus with aggressive social and political action (à la Gandhi and Gene Sharp).
- It sees no ethical problem in applying faith-rooted nonviolence to the public political realm (but recognizes the practical difficulties of doing so).

4. The Pacifism of the Messianic Community

Proponents include John H. Yoder and possibly Harry Huebner.

- This type depends on confession of Jesus Christ as Lord, sees nonviolent obedience as enabled through resurrection power and lived out in a distinct countercultural community made up of those committed to the way of the cross.

- It holds that the existence of such a human community dedicated to enemy-loving is a new moral datum, which will thus be a relevant witness to secular politics.

5. Political Pacifism or Political Nonviolence [Realist Pacifism]

Proponent: Duane Friesen.

- This type is similar to "Radical Pacifism" but with a higher degree of optimism about the possibility of effective nonviolent change in the world system; it also devotes more attention to secular analogues.

6. Post-political Pacifism [Neo-sectarian Pacifism]

Proponent: Ted Koontz.

- This type is a sophisticated return to a modified two-kingdom ethic, recognizing the moral necessity for occasional state violence but supporting nonviolence (even radical nonviolent action) as the Christian ethic.

7. Social Responsibility

Proponent: J. Lawrence Burkholder.

- In response to the Niebuhrian critique, Burkholder argues for a socially engaged Mennonite stance that would not be troubled by ethical compromise but holds to personal nonresistance.

8. Liberation Pacifism

Proponents: Arnold Snyder, Mark Neufeld, Perry Yoder, possibly LaVerne Rutschman.

- This type begins by standing in solidarity with the poor and oppressed.
- It emphasizes justice (perhaps as more primary than peace).
- It is reluctant to establish absolute nonviolence as a norm.

9. Nonviolent Statesmanship

Proponent: Gordon Kaufman.

- This type views unconditional neighbor-love as the primary principle.
- It may call for public political action that is contrary to personal conviction.

10. Canadian Pacifism

Proponents: Frank Epp, John Redekop.
- This type has much in common with political nonviolence and social responsibility.
- It sees the modern democratic state as a positive arena for Christian participation.

As noted at the outset, these are mere sketches, but I trust they offer enough to introduce the themes and open the way for further work.

A working paradigm of basic issues

The following is an adaptation and reworking of a document that I originally prepared more than twenty years ago for the 1968-70 Church and State Study Commission of the Mennonite Church, a group that included George Brunk II, John A. Lapp, Sanford G. Shetler, and John H. Yoder.

This paradigm attempts to bring some clarity and order to the way in which arguments and positions on peace theology (with special attention to church-state issues) are formed and supported. It seems to me that most of the major issues are still the same, many of the questions are unresolved, and the disputes go on. I propose that these items provide a framework for more intensive analysis of the various types introduced above.

T. Theological and biblical assumptions

T.1. The sovereignty of God.

T.1.a. What is God's ultimate will, especially regarding human destiny, in terms of love, justice, and judgment? Does God ever will violence or death? Is everything that happens in accord with God's will?

T.1.b. How does God rule the world? What does it mean to say that God acts in history?

T.2. The lordship of Christ.

T.2.a. Is Christ presently Lord over both church and world?

T.2.b. If Christ is understood as Lord of both, how is that lordship expressed differently in the two realms?

T.3. Biblical interpretation.

T.3.a. Relation of Old and New Testaments (and how God speaks in each).

T.3.b. How are ethical principles derived from Scripture?

T.3.c. Functions and limits of the hermeneutical community.

T.4. Nature and scope of the gospel.

T.4.a. How are ethics and salvation related?

T.4.b. In what sense is peace central to the gospel?

T.5. Eschatology: How does one's view of the end time affect peace ethics?

E. Ethical principles and procedures

E.1. One morality: Are all humans, including political rulers, governed by the same standard?

E.2. Is it ever right to kill?

E.3. Is the Christian ethic regarding violence best understood as nonresistance (ruling out both physical violence and psychological coercion) or as nonviolence (coercion may be acceptable) or as something else?

E.4. Are there legitimate sources of ethical insight, other than the Bible, for the Christian (e.g., natural law, positive law, sociological and anthropological data)?

E.5. Power and responsibility: How are they defined and evaluated?

C. The church

C.1. Relation of the kingdom of God and the visible church.

C.2. Priorities in mission: How are evangelism, justice, peacemaking, social service, etc., related?

C.3. Social form and strategy (church-type or sect-type or something else?).

C.4. Tension of eternal/temporal dimensions of discipleship.

C.5. Locus of authority and decision-making processes.

S. The state and society

S.1. Nature of the state: Is it a divine institution or a human structure? What of "principalities and powers"? (This may in fact be a "T" level issue.)

S.2. Ethics of obedience and submission: the Romans 13 questions.

S.3. Meaning and priority of citizenship. (See also C.4. and P.1.)

S.3.a. National versus global loyalties.

S.3.b. Participation or withdrawal.

S.4. The state as guarantor of rights and freedoms.

S.5. Legitimacy: revolution versus authority.

S.6. Sociocultural captivities and Christian discernment.

S.7. Nature of the international system: chaos, balance of power, or transnational network?

S.8. Evaluation of ideologies and forms of government.

P. Policies and positions on church-state issues

P.1. Patriotism and citizenship (see C.4. and S.3.): levels and kinds of participation and refusal.

P.2. Meaning of "apolitical": Neutral? Indifferent? Vocational division of labor? Prophetic dissent?

P.3. The magistracy: office-holding and responsibility.

P.4. Appropriate forms of witness to governmental authorities (from prayer to civil disobedience).

P.5. Criteria for evaluating public policies.

D. Decisions on specific issues (samples and examples)

D.1. War taxes.

D.2. Draft resistance.

D.3. Laws on abortion.

D.4. Foreign policy decisions.

D.5. Cooperation, fellowship, coalitions with other groups.

This is obviously more than enough to enable others to begin to test the usefulness of such a scheme. It should be noted, however, that other recurring themes are relevant to any discussion of peace theology. For example:

1. The importance of one's location: Canada, United States, Japan, Nicaragua, or Kenya.
2. The imprint of personal experience: education, professional role, international exposure, observer or participant in various political and social settings, etc.

3. The meaning and function of numerous dualisms: time/eternity, this-worldly/other-worldly, optimism/pessimism, order/freedom, love/justice, realist/idealist, already/not yet, particular/universal.

Ten Types of Mennonite Peace Theology

Type 1

Historic Nonresistance

J. R. Burkholder

Nonresistance: The benchmark

American Mennonites have traditionally expressed their beliefs about the way of peace in the language of nonresistance, a term derived from the teaching of Jesus in Matthew 5—resist not evil, turn the other cheek, love your enemies—and expressing their intention to obey that teaching literally. This witness against violence and warfare was demonstrated in conscientious objection to military service and in a quest for alternatives to violence in other areas of life.

The major work of Guy F. Hershberger, *War, Peace, and Nonresistance* (1944, with major new editions in 1953 and 1969), set forth the Mennonite peace position more fully than ever before.[1] The book included both Old and New Testament exegesis, the history of peace thought in the Christian church with particular attention to the Anabaptist-Mennonite experience, and contemporary implications of the peace position. This landmark study functioned as a foundational peace theology for all the major Mennonite bodies in North America. The denominational resolutions and position statements from the 1940s to the 1960s all reflect the Hershberger consensus, with no significant deviations.

Nonresistance for Hershberger meant "pouring out one's love without reserve, even as Christ poured out His life completely on the cross for His enemies."[2] Thus the word became synonymous with the way of suffering love as exemplified in Jesus. Although strictly speaking the term implies a merely negative stance, it came to be used to characterize the ideal of a loving and peaceable way of life.

In the Mennonite Church, nonresistance was taught as the only authentic biblical and Anabaptist norm, consistent with the non-political

---

[1] Guy Franklin Hershberger, *War, Peace and Nonresistance* (Scottdale, PA: Herald Press, 1944 [1953, 1969]).

[2] Guy Franklin Hershberger, *The Way of the Cross in Human Relations* (Scottdale, PA: Herald Press, 1958), 41.

two-kingdom theology of the Schleitheim confession. As formulated by Hershberger, the nonresistant ethic had implications for every area of life. Beyond personal relations in the Christian community, it was also the guideline for industrial, legal, political, and economic relations. Its normative expression included refusal to sue at law or to join labor unions. Nonresistance was extended to include positive activities of Christian service, grounded in a community of faith.[3]

The social ethic of nonresistance

By 1958, Hershberger had developed a comprehensive biblical social ethic, representing a "fourth way" over against the liberal social gospel, fundamentalism, and Niebuhrian neo-orthodoxy. The axioms of that nonresistant ethic included:

1. The church is a "colony of heaven," not a merely human institution, nor yet a mystical transcendent phenomenon, but real people self-consciously giving expression to the kingdom of God here on earth and in history.

2. Because that colony is a social entity, the ethic is strongly social, going beyond the typical limited personal ethic of fundamentalists.

3. The pervasiveness of sin and fallen human nature is recognized, in agreement with much of the neo-orthodox critique of the liberal social gospel. Nation-states and governments are outside the realm of God's perfection (a crucial sectarian affirmation over against Christendom).

4. The call to discipleship and obedience is much more than good citizenship or living "responsibly"; it is ultimately the way of the cross.

5. Nonresistance is clearly distinguished from nonviolent resistance. In apparent agreement with Reinhold Niebuhr, this position holds that coercion is as wrong as violence.[4]

---

3 This introduction was adapted from J. R. Burkholder's essay on "Peace" in the forthcoming *Mennonite Encyclopedia*, vol. 5. [Cornelius J. Dyck and Dennis D. Martin, eds., *The Mennonite Encyclopedia*, vol. 5 (Scottdale, PA: Herald Press, 1990). See also John R. Burkholder, "Peace," *Global Anabaptist Mennonite Encyclopedia Online*, gameo.org.]

4 Adapted from Theron F. Schlabach, "To Focus a Mennonite Vision," in *Kingdom, Cross, and Community: Essays on Mennonite Themes in Honor of Guy F. Hershberger*, edited

Hershberger's mature views are summarized rhetorically in the sermon he preached in his seventy-fifth year, "Our Citizenship Is in Heaven." Characteristically, the colony-of-heaven theme appears as the basic metaphor for an alternative community, a platform for the faithful witness of nonresistance. That witness is intended to make an impact on both society and government, but Hershberger warns of the continual temptation to engage in worldly forms of political power. He reviews once again the Quaker experience: "My own personal acquaintance with many of our peace-loving Friends, the Quakers, together with long study of their history, has convinced me that the Quaker influence for peace has been greatest when and where they remained outside the political power structure, and weakest when and where they became involved on the inside."[5]

Paul Toews has called Hershberger's work a "conceptual triumph."[6] For Hershberger, the New Testament outlook is entirely unpolitical, and he understood the early Anabaptists in the same light. Yet by setting limits on conventional political activity, this nonpolitical posture compelled a search for more creative alternatives in service and witness. In its practical implications, the ethic contributed to the emergence of a prophetic witness that had significant relevance for the political and social order. Toews suggests that Hershberger could thus be "both Mennonite and American"; political withdrawal combined with social reformism.[7] The radical two-kingdom theology enabled a whole range of social and political activity, so that Don Smucker could call it a "new Biblical social gospel."[8]

As nonresistance was stretched conceptually toward implications for every area of life, the Mennonite mainstreams began to move away from a largely withdrawn, self-protective posture into more active forms of service and reconciling ministries, toward larger spheres of mission and social activism.

---

by John Richard Burkholder and Calvin Redekop (Scottdale, PA: Herald Press, 1976), 43-44.

5 Guy Franklin Hershberger, "Our Citizenship Is in Heaven," In *Kingdom, Cross, and Community: Essays on Mennonite Themes in Honor of Guy F. Hershberger*, edited by John Richard Burkholder and Calvin Redekop (Scottdale, PA: Herald Press, 1976), 279.

6 Paul Toews, "The Long Weekend or the Short Week: Mennonite Peace Theology, 1925-1944," *Mennonite Quarterly Review* 60, no. 1 (January 1986): 56.

7 Toews, "Long Weekend," 57.

8 Toews, "Long Weekend," 57.

Patterns in church-state thinking

In the planning for this project, questions of church and state and two-kingdoms have been recognized as crucially important themes. As background for further discussion, it seems helpful to review some pertinent material. More than twenty years ago, Richard Detweiler analyzed the major documents produced by the Peace Problems Committee of the Mennonite Church (some of which came to be adopted as official positions of the denomination). In my judgment, this small book, *Mennonite Statements on Peace, 1915–1966*,[9] is still a useful summary of the main issues that continue to be debated, not only in the Mennonite Church but across the "Anabaptist-speaking" world.

Detweiler's outline follows:

1. Constant features of the peace witness
   a. Historical basis in the Anabaptist-Mennonite tradition
   b. Biblical and Christological authority for witness
   c. Attitude of nonresistance
   d. Addressed to contemporary issues
   e. Respect for the state as ordered of God
   f. Social order as fallen, rebellious
   g. War is sin, peace is the will of God

2. Trends reflected in the documents
   a. More elaboration of theological bases for witness
   b. Expanded to include wider areas of concern: from conscription to labor and race relations, capital punishment, etc.
   c. Increasingly forward-looking stance (i.e., proactive rather than merely reactive)
   d. Posture of confession and repentance; identification with social ills
   e. More explicit gospel emphasis of evangelism and reconciliation[10]

---

9 Richard C. Detweiler, *Mennonite Statements on Peace, 1915–1966: A Historical and Theological Review of Anabaptist-Mennonite Concepts of Peace Witness and Church-State Relations* (Scottdale, PA: Herald Press, 1968).

10 Adapted from Detweiler, *Mennonite Statements on Peace*, 22–32. In-text citations in the following paragraphs are to this book.

Detweiler also presented a more detailed summation of the theology expressed in such foundational documents as the 1961 "The Christian Witness to the State." His main points are summarized as follows:

1. Though it assumes a basic separation of church and state, our contemporary theology gives attention to how the church may carry out a ministry of reconciliation and witness in relation to both the world and the state. The earlier concern about holding office and voting has been absorbed into the larger question of how to function as a Christian in the structures of modern society.

2. "The nature and function of the church are seen as essentially distinct from, but thereby relevant to, the world and state" (37). The church, as a new order under God, is not just another social institution confronting or even threatening the state, but rather is a witness to the reality of the kingdom of God. The church has no power but that of the cross.

3. Witness to the state is seen within the framework of the redemptive purpose of God; it grows out of the claims of the gospel on all creation. Such witness, however, must be communicated in "middle-axiom" terms in order to be intelligible outside the realm of faith. That is, the state cannot be expected to understand the gospel language, but presumably can be addressed through use of "humanitarian norms of civil justice . . . which have their ultimate reference point in the redemptive plan of God" (42).

4. The lordship of Christ over the "powers" of this world is a basic theological premise for this viewpoint, although there are significantly different understandings of this biblically rooted concept. The differences have to do both with the extent of lordship and the eschatological framework for it. "Concepts of Mennonite peace witness diverge primarily at the theological point as to whether the locus of Christ's lordship is only in the church where His rule has been accepted, thereby delivering believers from bondage to the powers of 'this world,' or whether His lordship applies also to the whole cosmic order under the rubric of redemption. . . . If Christ is Lord over both church and

world, witness to governmental authorities becomes part of the gospel message proclaiming a new age" (46-47).

This issue is complicated by the related eschatological question concerning the subjection of the powers in the present time, between the victory already won by Christ and the culmination yet to come. Detweiler suggests that these views are not irreconcilable, but the differences have become quite pronounced in subsequent discussion of the issues.

5. There is only one moral standard for both church and world (including the state); the crucial difference is in the response to that standard. This conviction enables Christians to call "all of society, including the state, to account for its conduct in keeping with the will of God as made known through Christ" (49). This view rejects the dual morality implied in comments sometimes heard among Mennonites, to the effect that God wills a particular aggressive military action, even though nonresistant Christians should have no part in it.

Beyond Hershberger

What has been the reaction to "Historical Nonresistance"? To begin on a personal note: I still recall my dismay when, as a Goshen College undergraduate in 1951, I encountered this accusation in a provocative book, *The Dagger and the Cross*: "Hershberger . . . represents a form of pacifism that tends to withdraw from participation in political life into a kind of psychological asceticism."[11] (Two or three years later, I became a student of that author, Baptist theologian Culbert Rutenber.) I never took a course with Hershberger, but I well remember his taking a carload of students to Columbus, Ohio, to an ecumenical peace meeting where I first heard A. J. Muste speak. I cannot recall that Hershberger offered any critique of Muste. In any case, Muste soon became one of my heroes and mentors as I discovered the wider American peace movement.

The fact is that Hershberger himself was always open to new ideas. He kept a clear and consistent center from which to operate, yet adapted to changes and circumstances, and at times transcended his published views. For example, in the early 1960s he participated in meetings of the Southern Christian Leadership Conference and made an essentially positive assessment of the philosophy and strategy that evolved around Dr. Martin

---

11 Culbert Rutenber, *The Dagger and the Cross* (New York: Fellowship, 1950), 18.

Luther King Jr. Already in 1957, Hershberger observed that King's blend of Gandhi and Jesus appeared to be more of "a strategy of appeal and less one of compulsion, and thus would seem more nearly to approach New Testament nonresistance."[12]

From another angle, the basic "nonresistance" of Jesus has been significantly reinterpreted by John Yoder in *The Politics of Jesus* and more recently by Walter Wink, who deals with the Matthew 5:39 text itself.[13] These understandings call in question the traditional strict separation of nonresistance and nonviolence. Wink offers us a model of Jesus's "third way," neither fight nor flight, that counters the "psychological wimp" criticism. Yoder convincingly demonstrates the social and political relevance of Jesus in his own historical setting. Although these revisionist views can hardly be accommodated within "Historic Nonresistance" as a distinct type, it could be argued that they represent legitimate developments of the classic expression.

A more troubling ethical critique of nonresistance is found in another 1950 book, Paul Ramsey's *Basic Christian Ethics*. He scored nonresistance as an inadequate social ethic, unable to respond to competing neighbor claims or to the need to protect third parties. "Love not itself self-defensive . . . nevertheless will impel men to develop an ethics of protection lest injustice be done to innocent third parties."[14] Can the demands of justice and social responsibility be ignored in order to preserve personal purity?

Subsequent Mennonite scholarship has endeavored to address these basic questions of pacifism and responsibility. In distinctive approaches, Lawrence Burkholder, Gordon Kaufman, and John Howard Yoder offered extensions and new interpretations that made it possible for many others to continue on a pacifist path, even though nonresistance was significantly reshaped in the process. But to mention these writers leads us to the other chapters in this publication.

---

12 Guy Franklin Hershberger, "Nonviolence," in *The Mennonite Encyclopedia*, vol. 3 (Scottdale, PA: Mennonite Publishing, 1957), 908. [See also Guy Franklin Hershberger, "Nonviolence," *Global Anabaptist Mennonite Encyclopedia Online*, gameo.org.]

13 John Howard Yoder, *The Politics of Jesus* (Grand Rapids: Eerdmans, 1972 [2nd ed., 1994]); Walter Wink, *Violence and Nonviolence in South Africa: Jesus' Third Way* (Philadelphia, PA: New Society Publishers, 1987), 12-34.

14 Paul Ramsey, *Basic Christian Ethics* (New York: Scribners, 1950), 165.

Type 2

Culturally Engaged Pacifism

Lauren Friesen

The problem

The history of Mennonite ethics is a history of continuous struggle to reconcile the teachings of Jesus (i.e., the Sermon on the Mount, pacifism) with social, political, and cultural realities. The effort to live the ideals of Jesus has resulted in conflict between the individual and the church on one hand and society on the other. Mennonite responses to this conflict and to society have been varied. Some have advocated withdrawal from society in order to live Jesus's ethic within the confines of family and congregational life. Advocates of the Christian community's radical separation from society generally prefer to label their peace ethic nonresistance.[1]

Other Mennonites have regarded the absolute claims of Jesus (pacifism) as an impossible ideal, retained as an article of faith subject to various compromises when put to the test.[2] Still others have sought to hold fast to the ideals of Jesus while developing paradigms for responsible Christian participation within society.

These three positions are reflected, in part, in preference for certain words to characterize Mennonite ethics. Hence, some writers prefer sole use of *nonresistance* to identify a Mennonite ethic, though others use *pacifism, peace witness, nonmilitarism, amity,* or *prohibition against violence.* In recent years, the peace glossary has expanded to include *peace and justice*

---

[1] See, for example, Guy Franklin Hershberger, *War, Peace, and Nonresistance* (Scottdale, PA: Herald Press, 1944). J. Lawrence Burkholder also regards nonresistance as the normative term for Mennonite ethics but has been critical of nonresistant Mennonites' lack of concern for justice and abnegation of social responsibility. See J. Lawrence Burkholder, *The Problem of Social Responsibility from the Perspective of the Mennonite Church* (Elkhart, IN: Institute of Mennonite Studies, 1989) [reprinted in J. Lawrence Burkholder, *Mennonite Ethics: From Isolation to Engagement,* edited by Lauren Friesen (Victoria, BC: Friesen Press, 2018)].

[2] See, for example, Theron Schlabach's discussion of Mennonite responses to military obligations during the Civil War: Theron F. Schlabach, *Peace, Faith, Nation* (Scottdale, PA: Herald Press, 1988), 173–200.

and *nonviolence*. This struggle with language shows that Mennonites have not found one term adequate to encompass the whole of a complex ethic, its claim on Christians, and its implications for their involvement in society. Even where writers use the same term, their definitions may differ significantly. This paper will follow the trajectory of one pacifist tradition of the third kind noted above, an authentic Mennonite peace ethic that seeks to engage culture.

The Russian Mennonite trajectory

At the conclusion of the nineteenth century and the inauguration of the twentieth, a number of Mennonite leaders came "preaching peace."[3] This paper deals with some of those leaders and their contribution to the Mennonite peace witness as Mennonite antecedents to the "Realist Pacifism" of Duane Friesen (1986), the idea of nonresistance in Gordon D. Kaufman's theology (1979), and (less directly) the nonviolence and "Social Responsibility" articulated by J. Lawrence Burkholder (1989).[4]

The course of the Mennonite peace witness described in this paper begins in the 1880s with C. H. Wedel and David Goerz and continues into the twentieth century, with significant changes, with H. P. Krehbiel, Edmund G. Kaufman, Gordon D. Kaufman, and Duane Friesen.

Cornelius H. Wedel

Cornelius H. Wedel was the first president of Bethel College, North Newton, Kansas. Prior to that appointment he taught theology at a German Presbyterian Seminary in Bloomfield, New Jersey. Wedel published in German, and only a few of his works have been translated. Gustav Haury translated Wedel's *Sketches from Church History for Mennonite Schools* (1924).[5] James Juhnke's recent *Dialogue with a Heritage* (1987) has given English readers glimpses of Wedel's thought, and Juhnke has analyzed

---

3 Schlabach, *Peace, Faith, Nation*, 158–72.

4 Duane K. Friesen, *Christian Peacemaking and International Conflict: A Realist Pacifist Perspective* (Scottdale, PA: Herald Press, 1986); Gordon D. Kaufman, *Nonresistance and Responsibility* (Newton, KS: Faith and Life Press, 1979); Burkholder, *Problem of Social Responsibility*.

5 C. H. Wedel, *Sketches from Church History for Mennonite Schools*, translated by Gustav Haury (Newton, KS: Herald Publishing, 1924).

that thought in "Mennonite History and Self-Understanding: North American Mennonitism as a Bipolar Mosaic" (1988).[6]

Juhnke's analysis begins with Wedel's ecclesiology, with Wedel's understanding of the nature of the true church in the history of Christianity and the relationship of that church to culture. "Wedel's approach to the Christ-and-culture question [and hence his peace theology] was largely shaped by the influence of German idealism and historicism upon his historical vision";[7] from German idealism he learned a dialectical method. Wedel perceived a basic tension between free church and state church; this is his primary dialectic. A secondary dialectic deals with the relationship between Christianity and culture. Wedel's understanding of the free church in these two areas of struggle has influenced subsequent movements in Mennonite peace theology.[8]

Wedel believed the history of Christianity could be understood in terms of a struggle between the state church, which pays a high allegiance to the state, and the free church, which has a greater allegiance to the claims of Jesus. In his account of church history, Wedel observed a continuous tradition, which began with the New Testament church, included the medieval reformers (Priscillian, Claudius of Turin, Peter Waldo, and John Huss), and then found expression among the Anabaptists and Mennonites. Wedel called this strand *Gemeindechristentum*.

According to Wedel's first dialectic, God's truth has been more fully expressed in this congregational christendom than in "state christendom." State-church christendom is founded on and endures through wielding the sword; refusal to carry the sword is the mark of true Christianity. The fault of the state church is primarily its use of the sword: "The saddest result was that the people [at the time of the Crusades] began to believe it was a service acceptable to God to kill infidels and that it was right to spread Christianity with the sword."[9]

Mennonites constituted a counterculture over against the state church and participated in a tradition that went back not to the Reformation but

---

6 James C. Juhnke, *Dialogue with a Heritage* (North Newton, KS: Bethel College, 1987); James C. Juhnke, "Mennonite History and Self-understanding: North American Mennonitism as a Bipolar Mosaic," in *Mennonite Identity: Historical and Contemporary Perspectives*, edited by Calvin Wall Redekop and Samuel J. Steiner (Lanaham, MD: University Press of America, 1988), 83–100.

7 Juhnke, *Dialogue with a Heritage*, 84.

8 Juhnke, *Dialogue with a Heritage*, 56.

9 Wedel, *Sketches from Church History*, 36.

to the New Testament early church. Wedel held that one of the Anabaptists' distinctive features was their refusal to participate in war and military service; instead, they believed they were called to love their enemies.[10] Wedel's articulation of that principle did not stress merely obeying Jesus's command but instead emphasized embodying the spirit of Jesus's life of service. Loving one's enemies is not optional but imperative for those who refuse to carry the sword.

According to Wedel's second dialectic, *Gemeindechristentum* should be actively engaged with culture: the arts, literature, and culture should flourish. (Noah Byers, president of Goshen College, shared these sentiments; in 1904 he coined the college motto "Culture for Service.") Congregational christendom can withdraw from the structures of violence while maintaining an active engagement with culture. Mennonite theology must not be cut off from cultural life or from responsibility for social institutions in which Mennonites are properly involved. Mennonites should participate in culture and offer their peace witness as a contribution to society. In the same way that one can love an enemy without becoming the enemy, one should participate in culture without becoming totally absorbed by it. Christians can enjoy the fruits of civilization without losing their Christian witness; in fact, a viable peace witness requires that Christians live both in culture and in Christian community. Wedel assumed that an influx of Christians into social institutions would enhance the integrity and morality of those institutions.[11]

Although he emphasized that peace is the one essential distinctive for the true church, Wedel avoided use of the term *nonresistance*. How did he identify his peace position without using the word that has become standard, indeed a litmus test, for some Mennonite peace theologies? Wedel used various phrases and words for his Mennonite peace theology. Borrowing from Hans Denck, he wrote about "loving your enemies and prohibiting all violence," about Mennonite refusal to participate in war, to join the military, or to do violence against another. Service to society is an expression of the Mennonite peace witness. The work of Mennonite

---

10 Wedel, *Sketches from Church History*, 51.

11 The problem of the relation between Christianity and culture has interested people in the [Old] Mennonite tradition as well. J. Lawrence Burkholder's 1958 dissertation, written at Princeton, also examines Mennonite ethics and the problem of social responsibility (Burkholder, *Problem of Social Responsibility*). Though his work is apparently not informed by Wedel's paradigm, Burkholder explores the same fundamental problem: How can a church that espouses a nonviolent ethic be socially responsible?

missionaries with the Cheyenne, Hopi, and Arapahoe Indians is an example of peace witness through service.[12] Peace is a word of action and links the work of missions, service, and culture.

The backdrop for Wedel's peace theology was the Russian Mennonite immigration of the 1870s, which was primarily motivated by a desire to live in a land free from military duty. It was a given that Mennonites would go to great lengths to avoid military conscription—for example, leave prosperity, homes, families.[13] Wedel's thinking did not center on resisting military service (which these Mennonites had done successfully for nearly two hundred years); rather he stressed a witness of peace for church and culture.

Wedel's second dialectic also had implications for his philosophy of education. Christian education should not imply a withdrawal from the world. Instead it entails "vigorous engagement with culture and an eager embrace of issues posed by modern learning."[14] Those embracing the ideals of Jesus should be in dialogue with culture and society in order to live a vital faith and to communicate with culture. How culture was to be understood was a matter of debate at the turn of the century, but Wedel's view can be illustrated best by his academic program at Bethel College. Faculty members and students participated in literary society debates and dramatic readings and attended performances by Chicago and Kansas City symphony orchestras. By 1900 Bethel had two art faculty members. B. F. Welty, a music professor at Bethel College, wrote in 1904 that the purpose of music is not mere adornment but the elevation of the soul.[15]

Perhaps Wedel's definitive statement, written in the final year of his life, was a commentary on the Elbing Catechism.[16] Originally published in Elbing, in West Prussia, in 1778, this catechism was popular among Amish and Mennonites in the nineteenth century in both Europe and North America. Wedel's commentary quotes Plato, Socrates, the oracle at Delphi, Descartes, Copernicus, Newton, Leonardo da Vinci, Dürer, Rembrandt, Goethe, and many other poets, painters, and writers. His referenc-

---

12 Wedel, *Sketches from Church History*, 105–140.

13 For more information, see Lawrence Klippenstein, "Mennonite Pacifism and State Service in Russia" (PhD diss., University of Minnesota, 1984).

14 Juhnke, *Dialogue with a Heritage*, 81.

15 B. F. Welty, "Notes from the History of Church Music in America," *Bethel College Monthly* 9 (May 1904): 18.

16 C. H. Wedel, *Meditationen zu den Fragen und Antworten unseres Katechismus* (Newton, KS: Herold Druck, 1911).

es to the arts reflect Mennonite education and culture at the time.[17] The ancient tradition of the reciter—a community member who performed short vignettes and recited poetry, aphorisms, humorous quips, and anecdotes—emerged among Mennonites in Russia and stayed with them in their new land until World War II.[18] The aim was dialogue with culture without losing one's soul!

Wedel wanted Mennonites to remain bilingual. In America, English was essential for participation in the national ethos. But German remained imperative because it was the language of culture. In Berlin Wedel had attended church historian and liberal theologian Adolf von Harnack's theology lectures. He disagreed with Harnack, but thought that on many subjects there was "much to learn" from him. In any case, the experience reinforced his convictions about the importance of retaining German language. Wedel hoped that Mennonite education would result in Mennonite participation in the Enlightenment tradition of German culture. Until World War I, Bethel College offered instruction in German and English, and its catalogue was published in both languages.

David Goerz

David Goerz's was another voice supporting the view that Mennonite peace witness involves active service and engagement with culture. Goerz was a Russian Mennonite immigrant who on arriving in Kansas in 1875 lost no time organizing neighboring Mennonite communities. He was a businessman, educator, pastor and leader. A flour mill in Halstead, Kansas, provided his financial security while he founded the Herald Publishing Company, a railway ticket agency, Mennonite Society for Relief, Mennonite Indian and Foreign Missions, and a nurses school. He also wrote the charter for Bethel College, signed the first building contracts, persuaded C. H. Wedel to become the first president, hired many members of the initial faculty, and served as the business manager until his death in 1909.[19]

---

17 Compare H. Goerz, "The Cultural Life among the Mennonites of Russia," *Mennonite Life* 24 (July 1969): 99-100; and N. J. Klassen, "Mennonite Intelligentsia in Russia," *Mennonite Life* 24 (April 1969): 51-60.

18 For more on the tradition of the reciter, see Jerry V. Pickering, "Medieval Origins of European Folk Dramas," paper presented at the Association for Theater in Higher Education Conference, 9 August 1988, Chicago.

19 Material on Goerz's life is available in the Bethel College Historical Library.

Goerz was educated in Berlin and then (as a young man, before he went to Kansas) was employed by Johann Cornies, whom the czar had appointed as a sort of governor of the Mennonite villages in the Ukraine. During the next decade, Goerz refined his administrative skills under Cornies's tutelage; in his work for Cornies, Goerz moved among merchants, government officials, academics, journalists, and religious leaders. Because of this experience, later, in Kansas, he did not hesitate to work with local and national leaders to accomplish his objectives of building Mennonite institutions and communities. When Mennonite missionaries reported a famine in India, he launched a drive to ship the needed wheat. In a short time he collected 10,000 tons, received shipping permits at low cost and government approval for the venture. He personally accompanied the shipment.[20] Goerz established Mennonite institutions, communicated with civil leaders, expressed appreciation for culture and learning, and articulated a peace witness conjoined with service.

At the dedication service for Bethel College, Goerz flew the American flag—a gift to the college—from the front windows of the administration building. In his letter to donors, he explained that the flag in this context should be viewed as a symbol of freedom, liberty, independence, and good will toward all, and not as a battle symbol. The flag could signify freedom of worship for Mennonites in America, in contrast to the restrictions they faced in Russia.[21] His letter is a brief but clear statement about the role of the state and his view that even a peace church can reinterpret and use the symbols of government without jeopardizing its peace witness.

Directly or indirectly, the thought of Wedel and the activism of Goerz have influenced subsequent Mennonite thought on issues of war and peace, faith and culture, the relation between the claims of Jesus and social realities and institutions.[22] Because they wrote in German, their influence waned during and after World War I, as the use of the German language diminished among Mennonites. Nevertheless some leaders, notably H. P. Krehbiel, continued in their tradition, though he altered its course at points.

---

20 John A. Lapp, *The Mennonite Church in India* (Scottdale, PA: Herald Press, 1972), 47; Lapp incorrectly reports that Goerz's home was Henderson, Nebraska.

21 P. J. Wedel, *The Story of Bethel College* (North Newton, KS: Bethel College 1954), 87.

22 Juhnke, *Dialogue with a Heritage*, 105.

H. P. Krehbiel

H. P. Krehbiel wrote extensively. Works significant for this study are: *A Trip through Europe: A Plea for the Abolition of War* (1926), and *War, Peace, Amity* (1937).[23] The latter work includes a chapter by his daughter, Elva Krehbiel Leisy, titled "Women and Peace."[24] As the founder of *Mennonite Weekly Review*, Krehbiel sought to clarify Mennonite history and theology for the diverse body of Mennonites. As a state senator in Kansas, he attempted to interpret the political realm to Mennonites.

In addition to bringing news from Mennonites to his readers, Krehbiel was actively adapting Mennonite theology to two realities of American Mennonite life: social institutions and democracy. In hindsight, his statements reveal an outlook that frequently seems rose-tinted.

Lois Barrett refers to Krehbiel's pacifism as "Political Nonviolence," because he used political language to articulate both his theology and his peace interests.[25] Krehbiel saw separate roles for the church and Christian state, but each should, as much as possible, aspire to the same ethical standards. The church has different objectives than the state, namely, to "win the world to Christ and realize peace on earth and good will toward men."[26] The church should address humanity's spiritual, social, and ethical side. The obligation of the state is to regulate economic, social, political, and domestic affairs of the community. Christians are like leaven in a society and will slowly infiltrate all institutions, rendering them more just and ethical. The church and the political "fields" address different aspects of life—one deals with love and the other with justice (law). There is a line of demarcation between the state and the church, and Christians need to follow their conscience and obey God even when it may result in

---

23 H. P. Krehbiel, *A Trip through Europe: A Plea for the Abolition of War* (Newton, KS: Herald Publishing, 1926); H. P. Krehbiel, *War, Peace, Amity* (Newton, KS: Herald Publishing, 1937).

24 See also Kim Schmidt, "The North Newton WILPF: Educating for Peace," *Mennonite Life* 40 (December 1985): 8–13.

25 Lois Barrett, "A critique of 'Political Nonviolence,'" paper presented at the joint meeting of the MCC Peace Committee and Ecumenical Peace Theology Working Group, 3-4 November, Elkhart, Indiana, 1989. A more recent version of Barrett's essay, "Realist Pacifism," appears in the present collection, minus the section on antecedents to Duane Friesen's approach. That material is incorporated instead in the present essay; the editors decided it merited treatment as a separate type. I am indebted to Barrett's work on Krehbiel for many of the following observations.

26 Krehbiel, *War, Peace, Amity*, 188. In-text citations in following paragraphs are to this work.

disobeying government. The command to love the enemy would, in some circumstances, compel a Christian to disobey the state. Krehbiel assumed, though, that a Christian state can, if it wants to, live according to the principles of Christian ethics.

> If a nation will recognize and exercise in its individual, social, and political activities and in its moral and spiritual life a consistent obedience to the laws and injunctions of God as revealed in Jesus Christ, then will righteousness, justice, peace and plenty be the blissful lot of that nation. (268-69)

Embedded in that statement is the assumption that society can adopt an ethical system that is consistent with Christian ethics. This is not accomplished through direct confrontation between church and state, nor when the church as a body orders the state to take a certain stand. But Krehbiel did advocate that the church educate its members on these issues; then individual Christians could take positions as citizens and not as representatives of the church.

The church should inspire its members to political action (272). Christians should seek to make temporal laws that do not contradict God's eternal laws. Private citizens should lay down their arms to end the lawlessness caused by an armed citizenry. Krehbiel saw a role for the police because they operate only against the offender and not as the army (which is organized brutality against entire nations). He also advocated moving beyond world armistice toward a peace "where the spirit of strife and combat is absent . . ., where love, kindled by the spirit of Christ, has become the ruling force" (283). The way to peace is "not by the employment of violence. . . . Peace can exist and thrive only in an atmosphere of Christian love" (297).

Krehbiel apparently never used the term *nonresistance* but instead spoke of *amity* and *conscientious war resistance*. This is consistent with his political theology which advocates a Christian influence on civil authorities. He opposed not only war but militarism (laying up of arms), treating it as disobedience and repudiation of Jesus. He called for outraged consciences to speak out against war (301). In another chapter he referred to war as the greatest sin. He appealed for a revolution against militarism and an international call to amity.

Because he believed that a Christian citizenry will effect a more Christlike public policy and government, Krehbiel's political nonviolence was an active nonviolence. His attempt to translate traditional Mennonite refusal to do military duty into a democratic active voice for peace left only one choice: Christian peace activism for a nonviolent society and world. His was a peace activism that took into consideration the realities of the political order. Yet he was cautious and thought the church should not confront the state on domestic economic issues (labor disputes, wages, or taxes).

In his essay on the abolition of war, Krehbiel attempted first to analyze the causes and results of war, and then to establish a nonviolent response. The causes of war are simple: greed or pride, lying diplomacy, and militarism. The results of war are first, material devastation, and second, spiritual erosion. Truth is the first casualty of war. Children and women also suffer physically during wartime. He concluded that "a disciple of Jesus Christ . . . will say 'I have nothing to do with war, except denounce and oppose it.'"[27]

Krehbiel's position changed the direction of this Mennonite pacifist tradition. He analyzed government on its own terms and sought ways for Christians to make a convincing appeal to the state, an appeal that would affect the behavior of the state and make it more Christ-like. As Lois Barrett observes, Krehbiel did this without proposing that the Christian use "middle axioms" in witness to the state; instead, he wrote of peace and love as though they could be ethical principles for the state. He offered ideas for programs that, if realized, might result in a more peaceful world: an international law outlawing war, an end to secret treaties, institution of open peace pacts, universal voluntary disarmament, international arbitration, and a world court.

Krehbiel assumed that Christians' effect on a country would be to make its citizenry more Christian, more loving. This might involve obeying the laws of God and disobeying the laws of the state. And Christians might even find themselves denouncing the state for its militarism. The active nonviolence charted here was one that Krehbiel assumed would fit a democracy. He encouraged Christians to join with nonreligious people, such as other war resisters, to create a peaceful world.[28] Wedel's dialectic was still operative, but with a significant shift. The Mennonite peace wit-

---

27 Krehbiel, *A Trip through Europe*, 97.

28 See "Expansion of the Peace Movement since the World War" in Krehbiel, *War, Peace, Amity*, 316.

ness was no longer in dialogue with culture; it had now become an active participant, with state-church denominations, in shaping culture.

P. H. Richert

Other voices emerged, along the Wedel-Goerz-Krehbiel trajectory, that encouraged an active peace witness within the Christian community, in the culture and to the state. In 1942, P. H. Richert wrote a brief catechism that answered questions on war and military service. Though the book is primarily an exposition of biblical texts, the final paragraph is of interest here: "We are opposed to war as a method of settling disputes because it is unchristian, destructive of our highest values and sows the seed of future wars. We feel that we are true patriots because we build upon the eternal principles of right which are the only foundation of stable government in our world community."[29]

In the midst of World War II, this Mennonite professor of Bible could write about his opposition to war and about the foundations of stable government and world community. Here, in the midst of crisis, is an example of an active pacifism chastened by a sense of global responsibility.

Edmund G. Kaufman

Edmund G. Kaufman, former president of Bethel College, also wrote extensively on Mennonite missions and witness. He advocated a close connection between mission work and work for peace. For this former missionary to China, the Mennonite emphasis on peace implied action in the world and not a retreat from it. Limiting the peace witness to nonparticipation in war, he observed, had created a problem for Mennonites: "This non-resistant attitude has been a rather negative factor."[30] He used the term *nonresistance* but did not equate nonresistance with withdrawal from active participation in the world!

His solution to this problem has two dimensions. First, Mennonites should propagate the peace witness idea among other denominations. Second, "Mennonites should work toward a warless world in time of peace."[31] He called peace churches to unite in this "work toward a warless

---

29 P. H. Richert, *A Brief Catechism on Difficult Scripture Passages and Involved Questions on the Use of the Sword* (Newton, KS: [Western District Peace Committee], 1942), 20.

30 E. G. Kaufman, *The Development of the Missionary and Philanthropic Interests among the Mennonites of North America* (Berne, IN: Berne Book Concern, 1931), 114.

31 E. G. Kaufman, *The Development of the Missionary*, 115.

world" by establishing conferences, education and work projects, and by influencing government. Later he would write:

> Love must be inclusive so as to take in even the enemy. It must also be positive and express itself in concrete action. . . . The only way the reality of the peace stand can be proved to others is by carrying it out in action. It is through practice that it will be preserved. Too many times this nonresistant stand is thought of negatively, as "not" doing something instead of "doing" something.[32]

Kaufman's activism focused primarily on linking missions and relief work with peace witness. In joining these, he emphasized that the Christian church should live the peace witness in society (compare C. H. Wedel's *Gemeindechristentum*). An active peace witness will have an impact on global political realities: the nations of the world will become more peaceful and just, by following the example of Christian love. It should be noted, though, that the efficacy of the Mennonite peace witness did not depend on this transformation of nations. The dialectic that Wedel described between congregational church and state church, and congregational church and culture, was operative in the missionary and peace theology of Edmund G. Kaufman. He brought it most clearly into a global arena, with the emphasis on an active peace witness.

Gordon D. Kaufman

The most recent voice in this tradition is Gordon D. Kaufman's. Kaufman, professor of theology at Harvard Divinity School, has also been influenced by these earlier efforts to link peace witness and cultural engagement. Kaufman has examined the tension between nonresistance and responsibility to society. He has written, "Love is not that which keeps out of trouble, a means of remaining above and secure from the conflicts of this world. Love is precisely that which goes into the very heart of an evil situation and attempts to rectify it."[33] Christian relief efforts are not adequate to show this love in action. Responsible nonresistance does not

---

32 E. G. Kaufman, *Our Mission as a Church of Christ* (Newton, KS: Faith and Life Press, 1944), 59.

33 Gordon D. Kaufman, *Nonresistance and Responsibility* (Newton, KS: Faith and Life Press, 1979), 64-65.

end with charity, but delves into the foundations of society and calls for justice and love.

Active love, rather than separation from the world, is the true meaning of nonresistance. Love vaults the Christian into the world; there Christians try to act redemptively. To withdraw from the world is to fail to love, because Christian love always takes responsibility for the sinful situation.

For Kaufman, Christian responsibility has three dimensions. The first is a missionary task: to proclaim God's love to our neighbor (and to society). Second, Christians should seek to understand sympathetically the situation of our neighbor (and society) and accept that neighbor as a person (and that society as a society). Kaufman reminds us that we cannot expect Christian pacifism from non-Christians; therefore our appeal to our neighbors (and our societies) should be that they live authentically according to their own self-understanding and convictions. Christians cannot impose a Christian ethic on a society that does not claim that ethic. In the third place, then, Christians should encourage neighbors and nations to follow courses of action most consistent with their best ideals, even if those ideals do not meet the standards established by Mennonite pacifist ethics.

In one sense, C. H. Wedel's theology of cultural engagement reaches maturity in Kaufman's views. Mennonite pacifist ethics has not been compromised, yet a rationale has been articulated for dialogue and suasion between the church and culture. The position now avoids complete withdrawal from society (as some theologies of nonresistance advocate), or prophetic confrontation between church and state (as other theologies advocate), or Christian domination of state and culture (Krehbiel's tendency). In Kaufman's view, Christian love, nonresistant love, calls nation and neighbor to be authentic in their claim that they seek justice and peace. On the basis of this love, Christians can join with others in the political or cultural arena in a common quest for truth. "Radical nonresistant discipleship leads us into the world rather than away from it."[34]

The cultural realm of art, in Kaufman's view, should not be ignored as a place for pursuing peace. The modern artist does not attempt simply to create beauty, to make pleasing ornaments, but tries rather to reveal us to ourselves:

> If in Picasso's paintings twisted and contorted faces, human bodies broken to pieces, and images of chaos ap-

---

34 G. D. Kaufman, *Nonresistance and Responsibility*, 102.

pear, instead of disdaining what seems to us the disorder of his painting, we should ask whether he has not reflected and expressed in an especially vivid and profound way the destructive horrors of the actual world in which we live, which tears people to shreds in atomic war and death camps and racial hatred.[35]

Active nonresistance may thrust the Christian into society's heart of darkness. This is a redemptive act and not a compromise of ethical principles. The Christian should welcome it as an authentication of faith in the providence of God's love. Redemptive love transforms not only the believing one, but also, through nonresistant love, the world.

This type of pacifist cultural engagement is, in summary, a form of active nonresistance. Though it is lived in Christian community, it is in dialogue with other communities (culture, politics and society) in an effort to love, understand, and transform them:

> As it is . . . , many of a person's vital relations (economic, political, social) are extra-ecclesiastical. One lives in and is sustained by a variety of communities and owes much to each. One's life and responsibilities, then, cannot rightly be defined simply by reference to the church.[36]

Therefore, because of the claims of nonresistant love, the Christian is more responsible than the non-Christian for the conditions (justice) of society and the actions (peace) of its institutions.

Conclusion

Why did this Russian Mennonite trajectory either resist the term *nonresistance* altogether, or turn it into a basis for responsible participation in the political realm? Perhaps this tendency could be attributed to Russian Mennonites' understanding of the nature and necessity of political activity. Russian Mennonite perceptions developed in the context of small colonies, integrated communities with their own political administration. Colony organization covered all of life—not just congregational fellowship. It became obvious to Mennonites in Russia that justice is the ethical principle to use in organizing and administering such bodies, outside the

---

35 Gordon D. Kaufman, "The Significance of Art," *Mennonite Life* 20 (January 1965): 6.
36 G. D. Kaufman, *Nonresistance and Responsibility*, 107.

congregation. Even Christians who acknowledge love as the ultimate principle for human relationships need to sell land, exchange goods, impose discipline, and reward productive members; these transactions require the principle of justice. For those who share the whole of life, love, peace, justice, and responsibility are all necessary and inseparable, though conceptually distinguishable. Even culture was seen as inseparable from community life. The experience of establishing community institutions may have contributed, quite unconsciously, to the Russian Mennonite leaders' tendency to seek positive connections with cultural and political realities within American democracy.

Furthermore, it would appear that some Mennonites' proclivity toward not only literal but also legalistic interpretations of the Sermon on the Mount never had a significant impact on Russian Mennonite thinking. This is not to imply that this Russian Mennonite tradition consciously attempted to develop an alternative interpretation. It would seem, instead, that social realities gave rise to their hermeneutics. For Guy F. Hershberger, perpetuating a doctrine of nonresistance seemed to require separation from the religious and political institutions of the open American society. Wedel, influenced by the experience of Mennonites in Russia, assumed that a strong commitment to peace could be expressed with greater efficacy through engagement with culture and society.

Type 3

Social Responsibility

David Schroeder

J. Lawrence Burkholder's 1958 doctoral dissertation, "The Problem of Social Responsibility from the Perspective of the Mennonite Church" (1989), is a response to the call, issued by Reinhold Niebuhr and others in the 1940s and 1950s, for the social and political relevance of the church.[1] It is also Burkholder's attempt to deal with the dilemmas he faced as a relief worker in China in the years following World War II. He seeks to assess the degree to which the Mennonite church can comply with or respond to the call for relevance, and what aspects of this call need to be changed or rejected.

In Burkholder's preface to this recently published dissertation, he indicates that in the 1950s his attempt to come to terms with his China experience of moral ambiguity "met virtually no approving, let alone sympathetic responses from Mennonites" (iv). His attention to nonviolent resistance was dismissed as unbiblical, and no one wanted to hear about justice. He recognizes that "the delineation of the problem has undergone revisions since the 1940s and [19]50s when the sectarian ethics of the Mennonite church were still intact." But Mennonites continue to wrestle with questions about the shape of their social involvement, and his desire is that, however belatedly, this text "may yet contribute to the evolution of a mature Mennonite ethic" (iv).

Summary

Burkholder defines the problem by indicating that mainstream Protestant theologians are almost universally committed to Christian exercise of social responsibility. Mennonites, on the other hand, have until recently been satisfied to maintain their traditional "strategy of withdrawal" (23).

---

[1] J. Lawrence Burkholder, *The Problem of Social Responsibility from the Perspective of the Mennonite Church* (Elkhart, IN: Institute of Mennonite Studies, 1989) [reprinted in J. Lawrence Burkholder, *Mennonite Ethics: From Isolation to Engagement*, edited by Lauren Friesen (Victoria, BC: Friesen Press, 2018)]; in-text citations in this chapter are to this work.

But in the middle of the twentieth century, Mennonite "rural solidarity" has broken down, and Mennonites are increasingly aware of a needy world outside the bounds of the church (22). The church faces the dilemma: Do we try to turn our backs on the world in the interest of maintaining our separateness, or do we continue to risk involvement—with its moral ambiguities—in the interest of meeting the needs of more distant neighbors?

Responsibility involves accountability (*Verantwortung*), but for what, and to whom? Responsibility involves a general attitude of identification with the world, but to what end? Responsible Christian citizenship as described by Burkholder involves participation in civic affairs through the exercise of the vote, awareness of social issues, participation in political parties, and openness to political office-holding as a Christian vocation. Burkholder defines responsibility on the part of the church (drawing on Ernst Troeltsch's distinction between a church and a sect) as follows:

> A church may be said to be socially responsible if it seeks to produce a Christian culture including the political order, without necessarily stipulating how this is to be accomplished. On the other hand, a church which declines the task of Christianizing the total social order but prefers to concentrate on the church as a separate body, and therefore refuses to enter into the problems of society as a whole, may be said to reject social responsibility. (20)

According to Burkholder's analysis, the crucial problem for Mennonites today is that they have not come to terms with the impact of the industrial revolution on social structures. They have not faced the problem of love and the structures in spite of the fact that missions, relief and service, and education have made them aware of the world's needs. The radical sectarianism of the Anabaptists challenged the Christian civilization of the sixteenth century, but the Mennonite church is not a challenge to the world of today. At the same time, Burkholder claims, a policy of withdrawal is no longer possible.

In a section dealing with "the problem of Christ and culture," Burkholder describes Jesus as indifferent to the needs of the Jewish nation of his day (27). Jesus is seen as non-responsible, if not irresponsible. Jesus represents an absolute ethic which transcends any conceivable cultural system. This ethic is non-prudential and non-pragmatic because Jesus did not take into account the requirements of ordinary civil life, according to Burkholder. Burkholder's characterization here is that of Troeltsch and the Niebuhr brothers, but in my view, it does not do justice to the ethic of Jesus. Jesus lived in a society as real as ours, his words and deeds spoke to real issues and situations, and he challenged Jewish attitudes toward Rome as well as the validity of the law of the scribes. Burkholder finds Jesus' ethic wanting when compared to an ethic of "social responsibility" or of political relevance; in fact, we must judge the latter by the standard of Jesus.

"The entire approach of Mennonitism assumes the possibility of an unambiguous embodiment of an ethical ideal"; the approach is undialectic (31). That embodiment can be cultural; indeed, Mennonites have sometimes tried to establish a little "Christian culture' of their own" (31), though they would have condemned much of the rest of culture around them as evil. Is this a desirable approach? As Mennonites have become aware of broader social problems, they face the question: Should the church "seek to impose upon the political scene its absolutistic demands of Christ or should the Mennonite church speak with a 'wisdom' which is tempered by the realistic analysis of political facts" (31)? This dilemma is an outgrowth of the fact that Mennonites, according to Burkholder, are caught between the pure ethic of the Sermon on the Mount and participation in the normal processes of life in an evil society (32). "The clash between Christ's ethic and the facts of social existence are [sic] simply inescapable" (32).

The largest part of Burkholder's thesis deals with the central Anabaptist view of Christianity as discipleship. His excellent review of *Nachfolge* sets it off from Lutheran and Calvinist views. Special attention is paid to suffering, nonresistance, and mission. Each is seen as inseparable from discipleship.

The Anabaptists' break with the corpus christianum is also an expression of their concern for discipleship. The Anabaptists rejected social responsibility on the corpus christianum model, desiring neither to dominate nor to be dominated by society. To accept responsibility for the maintenance of medieval Christendom would be to violate "the very nature of Christianity as a free response to Christ" (104), which is crucial to the integrity of Christian discipleship. The Anabaptists' church then became a free church, an alternate community unconformed to the civil community. Whereas the corpus christianum seeks to create a unity between church and society, "Anabaptism seeks to drive a wedge between the Christian community and the unregenerate world" (117).

Burkholder notes that Mennonites have undertaken significant social service in spite of their rejection of office-holding or direct political involvement. Their emphasis has been that of opposition to war, and voluntary service to those in need. But Burkholder does not see this as meeting the requirements of social responsibility.

Burkholder claims that "the idea of the Responsible Society," the ecumenical movement's criterion for judging all social orders, and its norm for Christian social action, presents a challenge to the Mennonite church in the modern world (192-93). According to Burkholder, the theological bases of the conception of the Responsible Society are (1) a rediscovery of a Christian understanding of human nature ("Man is created and called to be a free being, responsible to God and his neighbor" [210]), and (2) a rediscovery of the biblical doctrine of Christ's lordship or kingship as extending "over all human authorities and institutions" (211). Burkholder asserts that the theoretical differences are great between the Mennonite church and the ecumenical movement with its Responsible Society ideal; the practical differences are not as great (212).

The Mennonites and the ecumenical community differ most fundamentally on the framework of Christian social ethics. For the latter the frame of reference is the entire world; for the former it is the church (the denomination, or the Mennonite community) (212-13). Mennonites acknowledge the universality of Christ's rule, Burkholder claims, but "they have never worked through the implications" of the doctrine of the lordship of Christ for social ethics (214). Mennonites limit the lordship of Christ to the church.

Burkholder comes to the following conclusions:

1. A fundamental conflict exists between the absolutist ethic of nonresistance ("the way of the cross") and "the relativities of the social order" (222). This conflict can no longer be resolved by retreat into isolation. Therefore, the Mennonite approach to society must be revised: "Mennonites must seek their traditional goals of brotherhood, peace and mutuality under the conditions of compromise" (223). Mennonites are part of the world, with all its ambiguities, and their ethic must take into account their involvement, their guilt, their responsibility.

2. Mennonite ethics must make room for power because all institutions are political (relying on coercion or force) to some extent. Nonresistance is no longer valid "as a comprehensive

norm for all Christian relations," because consistent practice of nonresistance "would literally take Christians out of this world" (223).

3. Mennonite ethics must redress its traditional neglect of justice. Mennonites' emphasis on love has led them to ignore this norm of economic life and goal of social action; the result has been confusion and apathy (223).

4. Mennonites must develop a new hermeneutic, addressing the problems of how literally Jesus' commands (or Paul's ethics) are to be adhered to today. "Until Mennonites produce a system of ethics which will have wrestled both with the essentials of Christianity on the one hand and the realities of modern life on the other hand, no final solution to the problem of social responsibility will be possible" (224).

Critique

Burkholder's call to responsibility fails to be convincing in a number of ways. First, he does not spell out clearly enough on what base the church is to be responsible and to whom. The Responsible Society idea of the ecumenical movement assumes a corpus christianum model which the Mennonite church has rejected as erroneous. The church must be the church. Its first loyalty is to Christ, not to the state or the culture (society). The call for the church to exercise social responsibility measures the church in terms of relevance to society rather than in terms of its truthfulness to Christ. In effect this approach asks the church to be true to the main tenets of a civil religion; the church is judged by its correspondence to what the society holds to be good or right. This is tantamount to giving up the Christian faith. Instead in all social settings the church is to act in the character of God as revealed in Christ. To do so could entail a critique of the prevailing norms of civil religion.

Second, Burkholder, in addressing the question of social responsibility, speaks more of individual responsibility than about the church as a corporate community. But the Christian is never merely an individual. The Christian is a member of a body of believers who together seek to discern the work and will of God. Through the church, as the church, individuals live and speak to aspects of culture.

Third, Burkholder is uncomfortable with the Schleitheim confession's contention that Christ's lordship over the church is different from

Christ's lordship over the world. Although he differentiates the Anabaptist position on the state from that of the Lutherans, he would clearly like to see contemporary Mennonites be more involved in what God does through the state. This is essentially the Lutheran solution.

I, too, have problems with the Schleitheim way of solving the problem. But my problem is that Schleitheim sees God working with people in two different ways: God deals with people in a violent way through the state and in a forgiving and merciful way through the church. I do not believe that God has a dual ethic. God relates to all people in the same way, inviting us to receive help through repentance, faith, and discipleship. The mission of the church is to proclaim the gospel to all people in word and deed. Christ has revealed the way God deals with people. It is a way of love, forgiveness, mercy, and self-sacrifice. This is also the way of the church.

Type 4

Apolitical Nonresistance

J. R. Burkholder

In the earlier part of the twentieth century, many Mennonites hesitated to be identified as pacifists. They made a point of distinguishing between their own commitment to biblical nonresistance and the pacifism of other religious and political groups whose position these Mennonites believed was based more on humanistic or philosophical views than on biblical authority.

One wing of Mennonitism, influenced by fundamentalism and dispensationalism, was critical of practically all efforts to influence governments toward more peaceful policies. These critics claimed that Christians are not called to prevent wars, but only to maintain their own nonresistant stance. Proponents of this view, fearful of what they termed modernist social gospel tendencies, also denounced Mennonite fraternization with other religious pacifists, including efforts to collaborate in public matters with Quakers and Church of the Brethren, as Historic Peace Churches.

Earlier voices for this position included John Horsch and George Brunk I, from the Mennonite church. At present, no one book or writer clearly embodies these views, but representative expressions are found in the publications *The Sword and Trumpet* and *Guidelines for Today*. Prominent recent spokesmen include James Hess, Sanford G. Shetler, J. Ward Shenk, and J. Otis Yoder. These critics have not advocated the overall geographical and cultural isolation of some earlier Mennonite leaders; indeed, they have shown a great deal of interest in contemporary social and political events. Competent observers suggest that their views reflect the opinions of many grassroots Mennonite constituents.

This group claims to uphold the traditional position of "Historic Nonresistance" against what they perceive to be a dangerous drift away from that position on the part of mainstream Mennonitism. Two major concerns are the advocacy of nonviolent direct action and the breakdown of a rigorous two-kingdom ethic of church and state. Believing that Mennonites have become too involved in worldly politics, this group calls itself "apolitical." The proponents see themselves in a corrective and watchdog role, on guard against the trends they deplore.

The following analysis of this viewpoint is based largely on a survey of *Guidelines for Today* from 1986 through 1989. This independent periodical was published monthly for a number of years and widely distributed in Mennonite churches. Sanford G. Shetler was editor until his death in March 1989. *Guidelines* was merged with *The Sword and Trumpet* in January 1990; political commentary since the merger is less prominent.

A typical issue of *Guidelines* includes inspirational or doctrinal articles in defense of orthodox Christian faith, news and critique of events in the religious realm (with special attention to Mennonites), and six to eight pages of social and political news briefs—especially items on moral issues such as alcohol use, abortion, and the entertainment industry. Much of the material is reprinted from other publications.

Guidelines probably offers more political and world news content than any other Mennonite periodical. The editor pens a regular section "On Church and State." James R. Hess writes frequently on public and political issues in his column, "In My Opinion." Many of the reprints and news items suggest a fascination with political matters. An extreme example is the full page of photographs of US presidents, with a key for identification (November–December 1988: 15).

Upholding nonresistance vs. nonviolence

Guidelines frequently challenges the shift in Mennonite ethics from pure nonresistance to acceptance of some kinds of nonviolent resistance and direct action. Beginning in the November–December 1986 issue, Shetler reprinted his 1967 pamphlet, "The Theory of Direct Nonviolent Action," in four installments. This extensive study of the Gandhian movement emphasizes the "grave differences" between nonviolence and the New Testament; it goes back to basic 1940s Mennonite documents to sharpen the distinctions.

Shetler follows the outline of Shridharani's *War without Violence*, with his own comments on each of the steps in this "ideal type" of nonviolent direct action. He emphasizes the claim that satyagraha is the "moral equivalent of war" and that, according to Shridharani, nonviolence is superior to Jesus, because the practitioner is not a helpless passive victim. Shetler states emphatically that direct nonviolent action "is not the way of Christ"; he laments that "high churchmen of our times have allowed themselves to be so utterly deceived" (July–August 1987: 10).

In a *Guidelines* column criticizing Mennonite involvement in peace movements, Shetler comments on the idea of Christian Peacemaker Teams:

> The most extreme humanistic program, being considered now by the Mennonite Church is that suggested by Ron Sider, a Brethren in Christ college teacher, who is proposing the idea of sending peace keeping teams to Nicaragua to stand between opposing factions. Many consider this not only extremely naive, but also futile in terms of bringing peace to that part of the world. It seems incredible that Mennonite leaders are giving any support to such a futile proposal. (March–April 1987: 20)

Theology of church and state

In 1988, *Guidelines* published a lengthy four-part essay, "Christian Citizens under Temporal Rulers," by S. G. Shetler, which set forth many of the key concerns and views that characterize the "apolitical" group (March–April 1988 through September–October 1988).

Shetler begins with an "overview" of various church-state theologies, opting then for what he calls the absolutist or purist position of the original Anabaptists. Using the work of Thomas Sanders, Shetler traces how Mennonites have strayed from that truth, noting the influence of J. W. Fretz and Elmer Neufeld at a 1956 Bethel College conference. He comments critically that the new theology of the "Lordship of Christ" regards the church "as an almost nonexistent structure which is simply part of God's good, big world" (March–April 1988: 22). This first installment ends with some critical comments on civil disobedience.

In part II, Shetler challenges the idea of "so-called prophetic witness" to the state, which he sees as a departure from the traditional Mennonite position. "That the church does have the right to communicate with the state is not questioned by anyone, but the matter of how and on what points are the focal issues" (May–June 1988: 22). Since 1965, Mennonites have become contradictory and ambiguous. For example, how can nonresistants dare to advise the state on what kinds of weapons are legitimate? It is interesting to note that in this section Shetler relies heavily on Paul Ramsey's critique of churchly political pronouncements.

With reference to the war tax issue, Shetler states that Jesus never raised the question of how Caesar should spend tax money, even though it must have paid for the soldiers who crucified him. Shetler calls attention to the critical political agenda and anti-American attitudes of most tax protesters.

Part III looks at civil religion and various forms of interaction between agencies of church and state. To those who would criticize the government's alleged misuse of religious symbols and language, Shetler calls attention to the other side of civil religion: the church engaging in politics or trying to use the state as its tool (July-August 1988: 22-23).

The final chapter summarizes New Testament teaching on Christians and the state, in nine propositions:

1. Prayer is to be made for all men, for kings, and those in authority.
2. We are to pay taxes and revenue.
3. We are to honor all those in authority.
4. We are to submit to every ordinance of man.
5. We are permitted to speak to men of state in the form of pleas for consideration and clemency.
6. We are in proper order to accept (not necessarily demand) protection from the government.
7. We are not to sue at law to protect our rights or to retrieve our goods.
8. We are to witness to temporal rulers concerning the Gospel of the Lord Jesus Christ and concerning their need for personal regeneration.
9. Christians must be prepared to accept suffering at the hands of unfriendly and evil authorities. (September-October 1988: 22-23)

The biblical command to "honor authorities" leads *Guidelines* writers to strong criticism of what they see as a "church press full of anti-Reagan statements." Shetler writes that a "great judgment rests on those who take lightly the Scriptures dealing with respect for civil authorities" (January-February 1987: 22). So it is not surprising that these men take a positive view of people in power. For example, in the March-April 1987 issue James R. Hess reports enthusiastically on his attendance at the National Prayer Breakfast events.

> I came away with a new hope and a new enthusiasm. Christ is alive and well and He is doing tremendous things in the halls of Washington, D.C. . . . President Reagan gave a short address. I was deeply touched by the honor and respect given the President. The thought struck me forcibly: This standing in his honor and all the clapping, is voluntary, not forced; it is not motivated by fear.

Editor Shetler, who also attended, noted that he found the total impact much better than many church conferences (March-April 1987: 11).

Guidelines thus grounds its views in the classic 1632 Dortrecht Confession of Faith. On various occasions its writers have quoted from Article XIII, "On the Office of Civil Government":

> We also believe and confess, that God has instituted civil government, for the punishment of the wicked and the protection of the pious. Wherefore we are not permitted to despise, revile, or resist the same, but to acknowledge it as a minister of God and be subject and obedient to it in all things that do not militate against the law, will, and commandments of God. (January-February 1987:23)

Summing up the "apolitical" ethic

The basic logic of *Guidelines* on church and state might be stated as "pray, pay, and obey"; the only exception allowed would be when obedience would clearly violate God's commandments. Some additional observations and implications of the *Guidelines* political perspective include:

1. The role of government is primarily negative: to restrain and punish lawbreakers; state welfare and social programs are often criticized.
2. Most Christian efforts to influence government are improper; Christians may, however, appeal for respect for the freedom of the church and for the freedom to live according to their convictions.
3. Some kinds of political activity may be acceptable for individual Christians, but the church as a body must stay out of politics.

This point is frequently made over against the assumed political meddling of mainstream Mennonites.

In *Guidelines*, concern for social and ethical issues focuses primarily on matters of personal morality: alcohol use, gambling, sexual deviation, and so on; the appeal is for change in individuals rather than for changes in public policy. Frequent admonitions appear against these and other aspects of worldliness: luxury cars, beauty salons, dancing, pipe organs, professional athletics. Although they often criticize domestic "welfare state" policies, *Guidelines* writers have not advocated direct political action to change such policies.

The world is generally viewed from an uncritical North American perspective. There is general support for the foreign policy agenda of the United States, along with sharp criticism of those church-people (Mennonites and others) who oppose American policies and actions. As Ron Sider commented at the November 1989 joint meeting of MCC's Peace Committee and Ecumenical Peace Theology Working Group, concern for social justice on a global scale seems to be lacking in the *Guidelines* agenda.

At the level of basic theology and ethics, the "apolitical" leaders presuppose a classic two-kingdom view. Although some of the leading spokespeople have denied that their position entails a contradictory ethic regarding killing ("What's wrong for us may be right for others"), one can find more than a few positive references in their writings to the necessity of lethal military and police action.

The peace ethic, therefore, is limited to personal nonresistance and conscientious objection to military service. The "apolitical" writers look with dismay on most efforts to persuade the government to act peacefully. They deplore Mennonite political activism. They question the claim that "peace is the heart of the gospel."

These writers also seem to rely on an eschatology that in the end returns political power to faithful Christians who in the present dispensation are to live nonresistantly. For example, Hess writes: "We who overcome and do the Lord's will to the end will be given authority over the nations and we will rule with a rod of iron, not with a democratic one-man-one-vote system" (September–October 1986: 10). Or again, commenting with apparent approval on the frequency of war language in the Bible: "When Christ comes back to earth as a ruler of a literal earthly kingdom He will make war on the nations, kill men and horses, and vultures will gorge on their carcasses" (May–June 1988: 11).

To accept the "apolitical" definition of proper peace witness would severely limit the public political behavior of Mennonites. To the question *Is our peace witness at risk?* the proponents of "apolitical" nonresistance would respond with a vigorous *Yes!* as they document the errors of political involvement and nonviolent activism. Although they do not hold many positions in Mennonite bureaucracies and institutions today, their influence may be noted in the "Letters to the Editor" departments of church periodicals, where grassroots voices frequently express these views. The overall importance of this position is probably underestimated by the mainstream intellectual leaders of the church.

Type 5

The Pacifism of the Messianic Community

Helmut Harder

John Howard Yoder has chosen the label "the pacifism of the messianic community" to distinguish his own variety of pacifism from others.[1] A summary and analysis of Yoder's position follow, using four representative writings: "Peace without Eschatology?," *The Christian Witness to the State*, *The Politics of Jesus*, and "'But We Do See Jesus': The Particularity of Incarnation and the Universality of Truth."[2]

Summary

"Peace without Eschatology?"

In "Peace without Eschatology?," an address given in the Netherlands in 1954 and published in 1959, Yoder dealt with the foundational question of the basis of peace theology. The address, coming after World War II, argues on the one hand against those who hope for a this-worldly "brotherhood of man" in the historical future, and, on the other hand, against those who view the war as precursor to an apocalyptic end and see no significance in historical events. In opposition to both views, Yoder commends the eschatological thinking implied in the Historic Peace Churches' use of the term "peace":

> "Peace" describes the pacifist's hope, the goal in the light of which he acts, the character of his action, the ultimate divine certainty which makes his position make sense;

---

[1] John Howard Yoder, *Nevertheless: The Varieties of Religious Pacifism* (Scottdale, PA: Herald Press, 1971), 122-27.

[2] John Howard Yoder, "Peace without Eschatology," a *Concern* reprint (Scottdale, PA: Herald Press, 1959); John Howard Yoder, *The Christian Witness to the State* (Newton, KS: Faith and Life Press, 1964); John Howard Yoder, *The Politics of Jesus* (Grand Rapids: Eerdmans, 1972); John Howard Yoder, "'But We Do See Jesus': The Particularity of Incarnation and the Universality of Truth," in John Howard Yoder, *The Priestly Kingdom: Social Ethics as Gospel* (Notre Dame, IN: University of Notre Dame Press, 1984), 46-62. In-text citations to these works are used throughout this essay.

> it does not describe the external appearance or the observable results of his behavior. This is what we mean by eschatology: a hope which, defying present frustration, defines a present position in terms of the unseen goal which gives it meaning. (5)

The basis of this understanding of peace is not only eschatological but christological. The eschatological foundation is determined by Jesus, who brought the new eon decisively into history. The incarnation, life, death, and resurrection of Jesus mark the separation between the old age of darkness and the new age of the light of the kingdom of God (6). Jesus announced an eschatologically oriented message and made possible a life of peace in the world.

Peace with eschatology has direct import for the Christian life of obedience. Those who confess Christ are called to separate themselves from the darkness of the old eon, and to live a life of suffering love in the light of the new eon. Jesus's followers find their identity within this same eschatological horizon. They constitute the faithful community, which, like Jesus, lives and suffers in the hope of the coming of the kingdom of God.

Yoder argues that a peace theology formed by New Testament eschatology nonetheless applies to every present historical situation. He speaks of a "peace witness" (16). Though an eschatologically based theology of peace is not dependent on or obligated to any this-worldly reign, it does call the world to change its evil ways. It does so from the vantage point of a community committed to its ethical principles, and willing to be faithful rather than compromise.

The Christian Witness to the State

This address from the 1950s serves as backdrop for Yoder's influential *The Christian Witness to the State* (1964). Going beyond the understandings implicit in the prevailing Mennonite nonresistance of the early 1950s, Yoder argues in this text that Christ is Lord of the state as well as the church (8-14). The messianic proclamation of Jesus, which was transhistorical, addressed the struggle between the old and the new eon. From this standpoint, Yoder challenges theologies that sharply distinguish the rule of Christ in the church from the reign of the powers of evil in the world, as well as those that hold dialectically that good and evil are mixed in both spheres. In the first case, faith has nothing constructive to offer the world; in the second case, compromise appears inevitable and legitimate.

Yoder argues instead that it is theologically necessary and practically possible for Christians to witness to the state about the state's obligation to Christ the Lord. The church's work is within history, but with a new understanding: the vengeance cycle can be replaced by "the creation of a new society, [the] aftertaste of God's loving triumph on the cross and foretaste of His ultimate loving triumph in His kingdom" (10). It is not necessary that the state see things this way. The New Testament views political authorities as agents of the divine economy in spite of themselves. The ultimate meaning of history is not in earthly empires, but in the church of Christ. Indeed, society functions and history progresses for the sake of the work of the church. "The meaning of history lies in the creation and the work of the church" (13). At bottom, writes Yoder, "the testimony that the risen Christ is Lord also over the world is to us the reason for speaking to the state, and the biblical witness concerning the reason for the state's continued existence enables us also to guide this testimony with definite standards" (21).

Although Yoder maintains one ethical base exists for both church and state, he acknowledges that the state will not conform to this standard. Realistically, the world will respond with "less than love." The Christian nonetheless witnesses to the state from the standpoint of the church's ethic of love and nonresistance. Christians must not accommodate their ethic to the state's limited possibilities. Christians must witness to the state, not take responsibility for the state by adjusting their theology to the needs of the state, nor judge that unless the state measures up to Christian standards it is useless to call the state to ethical responsibility. Ultimately biblical eschatology is the basis for the ethics of both state and church. Any difference between an ethic for the church and an ethic for the state is due to a duality of responses to the same Lord; it is not a dualism of realms or levels (32).

The Politics of Jesus

Yoder's next major preoccupation is with Christology. In *The Politics of Jesus* (1972), he seeks to demonstrate, by way of biblical study of Jesus, how "ecclesiology and eschatology come to have a new import for the substance of ethics" (5-6). As we should expect from his earlier writings, Yoder holds that a biblical understanding of Jesus must begin with his role as the eschatological Messiah: "Jesus was, in his divinely mandated (i.e. promised, anointed, messianic) prophethood, priesthood, and kingship, the bearer of a new possibility of human, social, and therefore political relationships. His baptism is the inauguration and his cross is the culmination of that new regime in which his disciples are called to share" (62-63). What Jesus proclaimed "was a new stance to be taken by repentant men in the midst of the world" (100), a stance empowered by its eschatological foundation and directed to the exercise of social responsibility.

What does it mean to be like Jesus? His community is nonconformist: "The believer's cross must be, like his Lord's, the price of his social nonconformity" (97). This posture of the believer creates community: "The personhood which [Jesus] proclaims as a healing, forgiving call to all is integrated into the social novelty of the healing community" (113).

How does one then move from the ethic of Jesus to the ethic of the community? In the apostolic ethical tradition of the New Testament, "one very pervasive . . . theme is the one we here may call 'participation' or 'correspondence,' in which the believer's behavior or attitude is said to 'correspond to' or reflect or 'partake of' the same quality or nature as that of his lord" (116). In this scheme "there is no general concept of living like Jesus" (134). At only one point does the New Testament consistently call us to be like Jesus, namely "at the point of the concrete social meaning of the cross in its relation to enmity and power. Servanthood replaces dominion, forgiveness absorbs hostility" (134).

Further, Yoder points to the New Testament concept of powers and structures (see, e.g., Col. 1:15-17) as a bridge from Christ to community. Jesus challenged the fallen powers and broke their dominance by refusing to yield to them or support their claims to ultimacy. This victory over the powers is the proclamation of the church, not only in its preaching, but more fundamentally in its being the new humanity in the world. The church must strive to avoid being seduced by the powers. Crucial here is the refusal to use unworthy means even for worthy ends. Instead, the church needs to see and believe that "the primary social structure through which the gospel works to change other structures is that of the Christian community" (157), under the sign of the nonviolent cross.

But the new community does not impose its unique way of living on society; it certainly does not have recourse to violence. Nor can change happen by embellishing or painting over an existing worldly order. Rather, the messianic community comes into its own by way of creative transformation originating in the messianic ethic of Jesus.

What are the implications for Christian attitude and relationship to governmental authorities? May followers of Jesus disregard such authorities? Or do texts such as Romans 13 require that Christians obey governments without question? Yoder answers: "The Christian who [following the New Testament] accepts his subjection to government retains his moral independence and judgment. The authority of government is not self-justifying. Whatever government exists is ordered by God; but the text [Rom. 13:1-7] does not say that whatever the government does or asks of its citizens is good" (207). Although Christians are to be subject to that historical process in which the sword is employed, they are not to order their own reconciling ministry by the sword (214).

How is the message of "justification by grace through faith" a foundation stone of the messianic community? Both grace and works belong to our justification. The New Testament is bent on the formation of the new community, made up of those who come with no tradition of works (Gentiles), and hence by grace alone, and those who have gloried in their righteousness (Jews), and thus also need grace. Because of Christ the covenant is now open to all. There is no longer any reason for hostility or vengeance. This is "the Good News that my enemy and I are united, through no merit or work of our own, in a new humanity that forbids henceforth my ever taking his life in my hands" (231-32).

Modern people want to make history come out right through our own strategic planning and efforts. Yet Jesus's teachings and attitude cause us to question whether this is our task. Meekness and suffering are not effective strategies. And should our concern be to guide the course of history according to what seems good from a human vantage point? Yoder observes, on the basis of the Revelation of John, that although God is active in history, "the relationship between the obedience of God's people and the triumph of God's cause is not a relationship of cause and effect but one of cross and resurrection" (238). This means that the followers of Jesus accept patience and powerlessness as their weapons.

Yoder ends *The Politics of Jesus* with a final hard question: "Does it make sense to ask the public authorities in civil society to enforce standards of fraternity and equity which Christians can seek after in the church on the basis of the free assent of those who claim to be committed to Christian obedience?" (246). His reflection on this question leads him to suggest that "the polemic of a valid Christian pacifist witness must be theological and first of all directed to the church" (247). It is preposterous to assume that the fundamental task of the church is to manage society. Rather, "a social style characterized by the creation of a new community and the rejection of violence of any kind is the theme of New Testament proclamation from beginning to end, from right to left. The cross of Christ is the model of Christian social efficacy, the power of God for those who believe" (250).

"But We Do See Jesus"

Although Yoder centers the obligation for faithfulness in the community, he constantly wants to bridge between church and world. We see this again in his significant essay, "'But We Do See Jesus': The Particularity of Incarnation and the Universality of Truth" (1984). Here he helps us avoid the dilemma posed in Gotthold Ephraim Lessing's image of an "ugly, broad ditch," a gulf between particulars and universals, between (for example) particularistic, historically based religious convictions and "the necessary truths of reason." Yoder shows us that we have no non-particularistic, supra-historical access to universal truth, that in the Incarnation the truth comes to our side of Lessing's ditch, and the attempt to cross it can be seen to be misguided.

The first mistake we make, writes Yoder, is to think "that the wider society is itself the universe" (49); any wider world we encounter is just another particular place whose categories we may use, though they give us no greater access to the universal. He points to the model provided by the Prologue to John's Gospel (John 1:1-18), which makes use of a proto-Gnostic cosmology. This cosmology shares Lessing's assumption of a gulf between the pure universal and the particulars. But instead of adopting that assumption, the writer of the prologue breaks the cosmology apart. Instead of interposing the Logos between the divine and the human, he puts the Logos both at the top of the ladder ("and the Word was God," the light enlightening every person), and at the bottom of the ladder ("the Word became flesh and dwelt among us," he came to his own and they rejected him). The concept of Logos has been transformed to carry "a proclamation of identification, incarnation, drawing all who believe into the power of becoming God's children" (51).

In the end one cannot do better than follow the genius of those who perceived Jesus aright in the first century AD:

> A handful of messianic Jews, moving beyond the defenses of their somewhat separate society to attack the intellectual bastions of majority culture, refused to contextualize their message by clothing it in the categories the world held ready. Instead, they seized the categories, hammered them into other shapes, and turned the cos-

mology on its head, with Jesus at the bottom, crucified as a common criminal, and at the top, preexistent Son and creator, and the church his instrument in today's battle. (54)

This, in broad outline, is how Yoder develops what he calls the "Pacifism of the Messianic Community." We turn now to some reflections on this particular type of peace theology, analyzing it using categories suggested by John R. Burkholder in his essay, "Can We Make Sense of Mennonite Peace Theology?" in the present volume.

Analysis

Theological and biblical assumptions

Yoder's understanding of peace is theologically based. His frame of reference, however, is not systematic but biblical theology, and particularly the theology arising from the New Testament. His approach is christocentric, focusing on Jesus of Nazareth as presented in the Gospels and understood in the New Testament as a whole.

Yoder, as noted above, begins with eschatology. But eschatology is not oriented only toward some future, end-time event. Rather the coming kingdom of God is the hope and motivating power of present faith and faithfulness, relevant to all of history. The characteristics of God's reign, known in and through Jesus's teachings, life, death, and resurrection, are the platform for the politics of the messianic community in its own life and in its relation to world, state, society.

In Yoder's scheme, ethics and salvation are of a piece. Jesus could not have accomplished our salvation except as the obedient Son of God; similarly the believer's appropriation of salvation occurs via obedience. Salvation embraces peace and nonviolence in the sense that since Christ died for all, it is no longer necessary for anyone to die for sin. Thus peace is central to the gospel.

Ethical principles and procedures

Yoder argues that Christian thinking cannot allow for a dual ethic in which one set of principles applies to the church and another to the world, one ethic is for Christians, and another is for others. Rather, because Christ is Lord of all, of both church and world, we must assume the same ethic is for both. We must not prescribe different ethical principles within Christ's domain. Yoder does not argue his case only on theological grounds. He reasons that the Christian ethic is, in the end, the humane approach, serving the best interests of humankind. Thus, the church should not compromise, offering the world a standard different from its own. The church should implore all people, and the state, to risk the better way.

The church

The kingdom of God and the messianic community are closely related, in Yoder's view. But the messianic community cannot be simply equated with visible churches. His church is a group faithful to the countercultural ideal of Jesus, the obedient disciples who dare to risk following in his way. The church, then, is visible where the works of Christ are visible. This visibility is functional rather than structural.

The church is evangelistic, but its evangelism includes—perhaps is even essentially constituted by—the gospel of justice and peace.

Yoder holds that so-called sect-type Christianity is closer to the true church (the messianic community) than is the church-type. In *The Politics of Jesus*, Yoder in effect maintains (against the mainstream Christendom tradition) that the Anabaptists were the true interpreters of Christian faith. At the same time, he argues (against some recent Mennonite thought and experience) that a faithful messianic "sect" need not be withdrawn from or indifferent or hostile to the wider world. The messianic community witnesses to the wider world.

The state and society

Yoder uses the New Testament rubric of "principalities and powers" to understand the state, as well as the world and human society. The principalities and powers are spiritual forces which, in their fallen perversion, are manifest in destructive acts, in subversive ideologies, and in unjust structures. It follows that the state is not evil (or good) as such, nor is any one form of government right or wrong per se. At best, the state exists in a tension between the temptation to evil and the calling to do good. This framework enables Yoder to see the line of demarcation between church and state in functional rather than official terms. Also, the state is seen as capable of hearing critique and responding positively to reminders of its obligations to do good (e.g., to protect freedoms, to shelter the needy).

Policies and positions on church-state issues

Although the Christian's citizenship is not of this world, a Christian may participate in the work of the state if such work is constructive, consistent with Christian faithfulness, and if one can sustain a critical witness to the state in the process. Further, there is a role for civil disobedience, provided one's witness is nonviolent and aimed at justice.

A concluding note

Guy F. Hershberger is the writer most often cited by people seeking to identify the Mennonite position historically prior to Yoder's own contribution. Yet Hershberger himself was part of the advisory group that in 1958-59 assisted Yoder in reworking *The Christian Witness to the State* in preparation for its 1964 publication. In this early writing, as in subsequent work, Yoder formulates his own understanding against the background of the Hershberger school of thought. In many respects, Yoder's work manifests continuity with the Mennonite peace theology of the past: in seeing the church as separate from the world, in understanding the Bible as God's revelation for all times, in regarding Jesus Christ as the foundation for the church and the norm for Christian life, in viewing faithfulness and obedience as crucial marks of Christian discipleship.

At several points, though, Yoder's position marks a shift from the earlier generation's peace theology. First, the earlier generation addressed the structured, visible church (i.e., the Mennonite denomination or Mennonite congregations). Yoder's work moves the emphasis to a more eschatologically based community; faithful churches are functionally but not structurally identifiable groups of people who obediently follow Christ's way in the world. Does the visible church get sidelined by this change in emphasis? Do we need a theology that takes the structured church more seriously? I raise this question in light of the fact that our current Mennonite peace work sometimes occurs with apparent legitimacy outside the church institution. At the same time, some Mennonite conferences and congregations question the inclusion of the "doctrine of peace" as part of their confession of faith.

Second, Yoder's "Pacifism of the Messianic Community" orients Christians differently in relation to the world. It is no longer a question of washing our hands of what is happening in the world. Nor is it a matter of providing theological legitimation for what the world does. Nor is it our task simply to rescue individuals out of the world. Nor is preserving the purity of the church as such a preoccupation. The Christian calling, for

Yoder, is rather to witness to the world concerning God's eschatological purposes for all of creation.

Type 6

Radical Pacifism

Barbara Nelson Gingerich

The working typology developed by John R. Burkholder identifies "Radical Pacifism" as a type of Mennonite/Brethren-in-Christ peace theology that "affiliates the rigorous nonviolent ethic of Jesus with aggressive social and political action."[1] The proponent of this position who has garnered the widest popular audience for his views is Ronald J. Sider. In his 1979 book, *Christ and Violence*, Sider articulates the biblical and theological convictions that underlie the activism he advocates.[2] Other major works that set forth Sider's thought include *Rich Christians in an Age of Hunger: A Biblical Study* (1977), *Completely Pro-life: Building a Consistent Stance* (1987), and *Non-violence: The Invincible Weapon?* (1989).[3] The analysis that follows uses the categories of J. R. Burkholder's paradigm of basic issues outlined in his essay, "Can We Make Sense of Mennonite Peace Theology," in the present volume.

Theological and biblical assumptions

The sovereignty of God

God's ultimate will for creation and humanity Sider characterizes as "the perfect shalom of the New Jerusalem," the peace-with-justice of a new earth, "the healing of the nations."[4] Sider does not explicitly address here the question of whether God ever wills violence, but *Rich Christians in an Age of Hunger* contains several passing references to God's destruction of people, rulers, nations, and institutions because of their sinful oppres-

---

[1] See J. R. Burkholder, "Can We Make Sense of Mennonite Peace Theology?," in the present volume.

[2] Ronald J. Sider, *Christ and Violence* (Scottdale, PA: Herald Press, 1979).

[3] Ronald J. Sider, *Rich Christians in an Age of Hunger: A Biblical Study* (Downers Grove, IL: InterVarsity Press, 1977); Ronald J. Sider, *Completely Pro-life: Building a Consistent Stance* (Downers Grove, IL: InterVarsity Press, 1987); Ronald J. Sider, *Non-violence: The Invincible Weapon?* (Dallas: Word Publishing, 1989).

[4] Sider, *Christ and Violence*, 96–97.

sion of the poor.⁵ His works also contain no extended treatment of the question of God's ultimate will in terms of judgment, though he denies that his position is universalistic. He does write that Jesus's cross reveals that "God's way of dealing with enemies is the way of suffering love."⁶ He quotes with approval Jürgen Moltmann's conclusion that "God comes not to carry out just revenge upon the evil, but to justify sinners by grace."⁷

Sin is a reality in the world, according to Sider; people and institutions and structures act in ways contrary to God's perfect will. But God will ultimately accomplish God's purpose to bring in a new age of peace and justice and is even now in the process of doing so, paradigmatically by means of an active love that is willing to accept the cost (suffering, death) of its confrontation with the powers of evil still at work in history.

The lordship of Christ

With regard to the extent of Christ's lordship, Sider repeatedly asserts that Jesus is "the Risen Sovereign of the whole glorious universe," "Lord of the world as well as the church."⁸ The difference in the way Christ is Lord over the church and over the world is underplayed; the continuity between his lordship over church and over world is accentuated. Indeed, the claim that Jesus is Lord over all of life is crucial to Sider's argument that Christians should work for changed economic relationships in the personal sphere, within the church, and in the public arena.⁹ Christians who reject this conclusion Sider identifies as theological liberals because they allow "the values of surrounding society rather than biblical truth to shape their thinking"¹⁰; thus, they deny Christ's lordship over all of life. If our confession that Jesus is Lord is to be authentic, according to Sider, we must hear Jesus's call "to be peacemakers through economic change—through more simple personal economic lifestyles, through more simple church lifestyles, and through action designed to change economic systems that produce violence by statute."¹¹

---

5   Sider, *Rich Christians*, 75, 136, 209.

6   Sider, *Christ and Violence*, 31.

7   Sider, *Christ and Violence*, 31.

8   Sider, *Christ and Violence*, 39, 56.

9   Sider, *Christ and Violence*, 81–87.

10 Sider, *Christ and Violence*, 85.

11 Sider, *Christ and Violence*, 87; compare Sider, *Rich Christians*, 225.

Biblical interpretation

Sider addresses some issues of biblical interpretation in a short section of *Rich Christians in an Age of Hunger*. Obviously, the way God reveals himself in Jesus's ministry, cross, and resurrection is decisive for Sider, but he does not explicitly attend to issues of the relationship between Old and New Testaments. He uses Levitical texts dealing with Jubilee, and prophetic passages on economic justice and divine concern for the poor and oppressed. Continuities between these Old Testament texts and Jesus's teachings are accented.

How does the Bible guide moral life? It seems to be for Sider a source of general ethical principles which then need to be applied to contemporary life.[12] Sider recognizes that the task of bridging the gap between principle and application is a difficult one, and Christians and Christian groups will disagree about the applications.[13] Sider does not deal with the issue of who discerns these principles or determines the shape of their application to our present situation; he gives no specific attention (in the texts examined here) to whether or how the church is a hermeneutical community.

Sider points to these fundamental biblical principles for structural change in society: "The sovereign Lord of this universe is always at work liberating the poor and oppressed and destroying the rich and mighty because of their injustice"; "God is on the side of the poor"; "Extremes of wealth and poverty are displeasing to the God of the Bible"; "Private property is legitimate, but since God is the only absolute owner, our right to acquire and use property is definitely limited."[14]

In *Completely Pro-life: Building a Consistent Stance*, a 1987 book Sider put together with staff members of Evangelicals for Social Action, he writes that "the total biblical story—the long history from creation and Fall through the call of Abraham and his descendants to Christ, the church and the Second Coming—shapes every aspect of Christian ethics, including politics." Here stress is not so much on discerning biblical principles as on bringing together the different strands of biblical thought on an issue and developing "a comprehensive summary or paradigm of biblical teaching" on that subject which then issues in an "articulation of

---

12 See Sider, *Rich Christians*, 95, 205-210.

13 See Sider, *Rich Christians*, 95, 210.

14 See Sider, *Rich Christians*, 95, 209.

a balanced biblical agenda of concerns."[15] This exercise in careful biblical study is only one of four steps Sider identifies in moving from the Bible to public policy proposals.[16]

Nature and scope of the gospel

Sider's treatment of the atonement displays his convictions about the connections between salvation and ethics. Rejecting the "weak sentimentality of the lowly Nazarene viewed merely as a noble martyr to truth and peace," Sider stresses Jesus's vicarious atonement, a unique, once-and-for-all, unrepeatable sacrifice for the sins of the world. This death demonstrates that God is "a merciful Father who reconciles His enemies through self-sacrificial love."[17] The bridge to ethics follows: in the cross, New Testament Christians discerned "a decisive ethical clue" for Christians' approach to their enemies as well.[18] On the one hand, according to Sider, Jesus's death is a unique, vicarious sacrifice which saves God's enemies (us) from our sins; on the other hand, his cross is a pattern or model for Christian response to enemies.

Without elaborating further the connection between these two convictions about Christ's atonement (as expiation and as example), Sider nonetheless maintains that to opt for one or the other would be to deny the full truth of the gospel. "It is a tragedy of our time," Sider suggests, "that many . . . who appropriate the biblical understanding of Christ's vicarious cross fail to see its direct implications for the problem of war and violence. And it is equally tragic," he asserts, "that some of those who most emphasize pacifism and non-violence fail to ground it in Christ's vicarious atonement."[19]

Peace and salvation are crucially linked in Sider's theology; violence and sin are similarly closely connected. Sin has two dimensions in Sider's thought. It is both "consciously willed, individual acts," and also "participation in evil social structures."[20] Sider perceives that most Christians are more preoccupied with the former than the latter, and he tries to redress the balance by calling attention to what he describes as the biblical

---

15 Sider, *Completely Pro-life*, 22-23.

16 Sider, *Completely Pro-life*, 21-24.

17 Sider, *Christ and Violence*, 35.

18 Sider, *Christ and Violence*, 35.

19 Sider, *Christ and Violence*, 34-35.

20 Sider, *Christ and Violence*, 70; compare 70-73 with Sider, *Rich Christians*, 133-37.

teaching on institutionalized violence, and Christians' participation in violent social structures today—in oppressive international trade patterns, in consumption of nonrenewable resources, in our eating patterns.[21] This structural evil is more subtle than personal sin, according to Sider, but it harms more people and is just as sinful as intentional acts are.

Eschatology

How does Sider's view of the endtime affect his peace ethics? It is the resurrection that provides for Sider the clearest indication of the relationship between our efforts on behalf of peace and justice now and the coming of the peaceable kingdom in its fullness. As there is both continuity and discontinuity between Jesus of Nazareth and the risen Christ, so there is continuity and discontinuity between our work now and the coming of the new age. Sider denies the liberal belief in a simple continuity: "We will not create more and more just societies until we . . . discover that the millennium has arrived."[22] But some continuity does exist: the consummation we await is not otherworldly but will be the restoration of this creation. Sider sums up: "So we work for justice and peace now, not with a naive optimism that forgets that faithfulness involves the cross, but with the solid assurance that the final word is resurrection."[23]

In a similar vein, *Rich Christians* concludes with this challenge: "If at this moment in history a few million Christians in affluent nations dare to join hands with the poor around the world, we will decisively influence the course of world history." And a reminder of the resurrection theme: "The resurrection of Jesus is our guarantee that . . . the final victory will surely come. Secure on that solid rock, we will plunge into this unjust world, changing now all we can and knowing that the Risen King will complete the victory."[24]

Ethical principles and procedures

As noted above in comments on Sider's downplaying of any difference between how Christ is Lord of the church and of the world, no ethical dualism is evident here. The same morality applies to everyone, to Christians and others, in the personal sphere and in the public arena. Sider acknowl-

---

21 See Sider, *Rich Christians*, 73–74.

22 Sider, *Christ and Violence*, 97.

23 Sider, *Christ and Violence*, 97.

24 See Sider, *Rich Christians*, 225–26; compare Sider, *Completely Pro-life*, 17–20.

edges that secular society does in fact have values and norms that do not cohere with those of Christian faith, but he does not believe Christians should endorse a standard for American society that falls short of the one Christians know by revelation.

In *Rich Christians* Sider explicitly addresses the issue of applying a single, biblically derived standard to both church and society. The church should first conform its own life to this standard, so our appeal to government for structural change will have integrity. These same biblical principles should then be applied to society because, far from being arbitrary, they are the principles that will produce peace and happiness for all God's creatures. "Following biblical principles on justice is the only way to lasting peace and social harmony for all human societies."[25] Though secular societies will only approximate the standard, the closer their approximation of it, the greater the peace, harmony, and happiness they will experience. Ultimately, we apply the same standard to both church and society because God does: "Yahweh applies the same standards of social justice to all."[26]

In his chapter on peacemaking and economics in *Christ and Violence*, Sider urges Christians to work for justice in the public arena. Because the worst violence—most harmful to most people—is structural, Christians should undertake to change unjust structures and make them just. Presumably this is the same justice we are to pursue in our personal lives and in our church life. Specific public policy recommendations appear under such general exhortations as: "We must demand a foreign policy that unequivocally sides with the poor" and "U.S. foreign policy ought to encourage justice."[27] Sider seems to regard change in structures as primarily a matter of changing what the government does—changes in law, in public policy, in foreign affairs. The standard for Christians and for government seems to be the same, and no allowance is made for differences of response; belief and the Holy Spirit's enablement are not taken into account in determining what is prescribed for whom.

Sider does not specifically address here the question of whether government can properly use lethal force, but his bias seems to be against conceding the propriety of such force. Sider's 1989 book, *Non-Violence: The Invincible Weapon?*, advocates exploring nonviolent alternatives to le-

---

25 See Sider, *Rich Christians*, 206.

26 See Sider, *Rich Christians*, 206.

27 Sider, *Christ and Violence*, 84.

thal violence in three areas: police work, national self-defense and international peacekeeping, and "middle-level situations demanding conflict resolution."[28] He considers it at least hypothetically possible that government could function without recourse to killing. Again, no difference, ultimately or provisionally, in what is prescribed for whom.

In *Christ and Violence*, Sider identifies nonresistance as the belief that Jesus's words in the Sermon on the Mount prohibit the Christian's use of coercion of any kind, whether violent or not. Though he acknowledges that this position has some value, Sider argues that even Christians who espouse nonresistance in fact act coercively in some relationships (e.g., parental and church discipline). Also, on biblical grounds, "the use of economic and political power is fully compatible with the way of the cross. . . . Activist nonviolence rather than nonresistance is the more faithful application of New Testament teaching."[29] Indeed, Sider's position might as well be labeled "Activist Nonviolence" as "Radical Pacifism."

For Sider the key distinction between "good" and "bad" coercion is the distinction between coercion that loves and respects "the other person as a free moral agent responsible to the Creator," and coercion that does not.[30] Wrong coercion treats the other as a thing rather than as a person; proper coercion has love as its goal and as its means.[31] The other's good (not one's own rights or needs) is decisive.[32]

On the question of other, nonbiblical sources of ethical insight, Sider claims that "the Christian dare not choose between a creation ethic and a kingdom ethic."[33] At the same time, he maintains that the fallen creation is now so corrupt that we cannot reliably derive ethical norms merely from looking at it. "Epistemologically our ethic will be a revealed ethic. But ontologically it must also be a creation ethic or we . . . forget that this fallen creation will ultimately be redeemed."[34]

Sider draws his definition of power from Max Weber: It is "the probability that one actor within a social relationship will be in a position to carry out his [or her!] own will despite resistance, regardless of the basis on

---

28 Sider, *Non-violence: The Invincible Weapon?*, 4.

29 Sider, *Christ and Violence*, 44.

30 Sider, *Christ and Violence*, 45.

31 Sider, *Christ and Violence*, 46.

32 Sider, *Christ and Violence*, 48.

33 Sider, *Christ and Violence*, 55.

34 Sider, *Christ and Violence*, 55.

which that probability rests.'"[35] Sider seems to use the word power interchangeably with coercion and force. As indicated above, the use of power/coercion is not itself wrong; it can be good or evil, depending on whether its use is controlled by love and concern for the "enemy."

Sider examines Matthew 5:39, the classic text used by advocates of nonresistance, and concludes, by looking at several incidents in Jesus's life, that Jesus cannot have been advocating absolute nonresistance to evil.[36] Jesus's cleansing of the temple and his response when struck on the cheek during his trial seem to Sider to demonstrate that "Do not resist one who is evil" means one should not exact equal damages for injury suffered, and one should not treat the injuring party as an enemy; one's first concern should always be for the good of the other.

Drawing on works by John Howard Yoder, Hendrik Berkhof, Richard Mouw, and others, Sider's analysis of power then turns to the Pauline categories of principalities and powers.[37] Not innately evil, these powers Sider understands as parts of God's good but fallen and rebellious creation. Sider believes the powers will not be destroyed in the end but will ultimately be disarmed and submissive to their creator and Lord. His analysis of the principalities and powers in Paul's writings confirms his conclusions based on his interpretation of Jesus's life and teachings on the subject of resisting evil: "Power itself is not innately evil. It is part of the good creation. Hence it can and should be used by Christians in loving nonviolent ways in the search for justice."[38]

The church

Perhaps the clearest statement of Sider's understanding of what the relationship between the kingdom of God and the church should be comes in the closing pages of *Christ and Violence*. Here he lapses into the familiar cadences of Martin Luther King Jr.'s "I Have a Dream" speech, himself dreaming of a time when the church's connectedness to the coming kingdom will be more evident. He does not picture the church as it actually is, but holds up an image of the church as it could be: "I dream of a time when thousands of congregations . . . have been transformed from comfortable clubs largely conforming to surrounding society's materialism

---

[35] Sider, *Christ and Violence*, 44; Sider's interpolation.

[36] Sider, *Christ and Violence*, 46–49.

[37] Sider, *Christ and Violence*, 49–58.

[38] Sider, *Christ and Violence*, 55.

into radical beachheads of the coming kingdom."[39] These groups would be "visible models of the coming shalom" whose wholeness "is so tangible and contagious that it will draw unbelievers to faith."[40] A parallel statement comes from *Rich Christians*: "The present quality of life among the people of God is to be a sign of that coming perfection and justice which will be revealed when the kingdoms of this world . . . become the kingdom of our Lord."[41]

How does Sider see the church's social form or strategy? On one hand, Sider's writings have a clear sectarian strain. Insofar as the church is faithful to the coming kingdom, it will be a countercultural, culture-critical body. Sider's normative church is a cognitive minority, a community of loving defiance, in which members are unconditionally accountable to and unlimitedly liable for each other.[42] Their fundamental convictions, their values, will be derived from scriptural norms and will put them in tension with society's prevailing values. This kind of body, to sustain itself in its radicalism, must be small, intimate: a house church, a commune, a congregation of house churches.[43]

Sider's primary critique of North American churches is that they fail to correspond to this sectarian norm: they are "comfortable clubs of conformity,"[44] allowing "the values of surrounding society rather than biblical truth to shape their thinking and acting," especially in economic matters, in relation to issues of poverty and justice.[45]

With regard to the question of the church's priorities in mission, Sider recognizes the missionary significance of the mere existence of faithful communities: "Precisely this incarnation of the new reality of the people of God will be a profound political act"[46]; "the church's very existence represents a fundamental challenge to surrounding society."[47]

But Sider is not content to stop with this kind of sectarian vision; it is not enough for the church to exemplify faithfully in its own life the way

---

39 Sider, *Christ and Violence*, 97.
40 Sider, *Christ and Violence*, 98.
41 Sider, *Rich Christians*, 87.
42 Sider, *Rich Christians*, 189–93.
43 Sider, *Rich Christians*, 195–202.
44 Sider, *Rich Christians*, 189.
45 Sider, *Christ and Violence*, 85.
46 Sider, *Christ and Violence*, 56.
47 Sider, *Christ and Violence*, 63.

of the coming kingdom. If the Christian community is to be sectarian, it is to be transformationist in its sectarianism: "The church as new community is no substitute for vigorous political engagement. Sophisticated, patient, political activity is imperative."[48] Sider even hints that focusing on building the church per se was a second-best option forced on Jesus by the intolerance of the political system under which he lived. In contrast to those Mennonites who believe that God works primarily through the faithful church, Sider seems convinced that the really vital arena of God's work is structural, governmental. He tells us:

> In [Jesus's] historical context, there was no political stance tolerated by the ruling dictatorship other than that of building a new community based on different values. That is exactly what He did. . . . Not every historical context permits political activity . . . directed toward the creation of more just social structures in secular society. When the historical context does not permit that kind of political activity, then obviously it is not an obligation. In a democratic society, political activity designed to promote structural change is possible. . . . I urge that we move forward creatively and boldly in the exercise of economic and political power. We need to become co-workers with the oppressed as they rightly search for a more just distribution of power in our world.[49]

So Sider's prime missionary agenda is for the church to become faithful and then to create in wider society more just socioeconomic structures, by nonviolent means. Using peaceable methods, faithful Christians will thus bring into being a more peaceful social order. Sider believes such efforts will be successful: if we return to the New Testament vision, "the Lord of the church may again create communities of loving defiance able to withstand and conquer powerful, pagan civilizations of East and West worshiping at the shrine of Mammon"[50]; "If we are wise and faithful, we can impact our nation and the world in a crucial way in the last fifteen

---

48 Sider, *Completely Pro-life*, 200.

49 Sider, *Christ and Violence*, 61–62.

50 Sider, *Rich Christians*, 202.

years of this millennium."⁵¹ There is something triumphal, perhaps even Constantinian, about this sectarianism.

Sider states his belief that such social change is not a substitute for evangelism. Maximum impact on society requires that we maintain a balance between evangelism and social concern, because "only redeeming grace" can "get to the root of selfish personalities"; "mere societal engineering [cannot] create new persons."⁵² This idea is noted only in passing and receives relatively little attention in Sider's work, perhaps because he feels his readers on the whole tip the balance in the direction of personal evangelism, and he needs to shift their attention to issues of justice.

The state and society

Sider believes that government is one of the powers created by God to order human society. In his view, "government is not merely a necessity because of the Fall"; it is "desirable for human existence, not just fallen human existence."⁵³ It is a divine institution, an order of creation, not merely a product of human civilization. As government predated the Fall, so in the end it will be restored, made incapable of doing evil, reconciled to God. This prelapsarian view of the state, and Sider's conviction that government will continue to exist when the kingdom comes in its fullness, accounts in part for his stress on engagement with government, and for his optimism about effecting substantial change in governmental policies.

The state, like the other powers, is fallen, but as a result of his crucifixion and resurrection Jesus has become its Lord. Far from owing the state uncritical obedience, those who know Jesus is Lord of all must announce that lordship to governments, telling them they are not sovereign, but are summoned by the risen Christ "to do justice, to seek peace, to promote shalom on earth."⁵⁴ This is a high view indeed of the calling of the state, at the opposite extreme from those Christian views that see the state almost exclusively as a curb on evil made necessary by human sin.

Following C. E. B. Cranfield and John Howard Yoder, Sider understands Romans 13 to enjoin subjection to government, but not absolute obedience. "Whenever government command[s] what [is] contrary

---

51 Sider, *Completely Pro-life*, 197.
52 Sider, *Completely Pro-life*, 22-23, 198.
53 Sider, *Christ and Violence*, 52.
54 Sider, *Christ and Violence*, 57.

to God's command, it must be disobeyed."⁵⁵ The New Testament does not sanction violent rebellion. Instead, Christians accept "the penalty for their disobedience," acknowledging government's real but limited authority over them.⁵⁶

On one hand, Sider's normative state seems to be a liberal democratic institution, safeguarding people's rights to liberty: "religious freedom, political freedom, due process of law and a pluralistic democratic process."⁵⁷ He shares Jerry Falwell's view that "biblical principles summon Christians to a ringing endorsement of freedom"; "I believe deeply that biblical values point toward the freedom of democracy rather than the slavery of totalitarianism."⁵⁸ On the other hand, in addition to guaranteeing freedoms, the state, in Sider's view, should be an instrument of justice. Sider's understanding of justice is not merely procedural; it is substantive, concerned with positive rights: more equitable distribution of wealth, fair trade, improving the lot of poor people. It is this balancing of concern for both freedom and justice, for negative and positive rights, that seems to define for Sider the good state: "One crucial test of whether Christian political activity is free of ideological bias from both left and right will be whether it emphasizes both freedom and justice in equal measure."⁵⁹

Church-state issues

Sider regards a wide range of forms of witness to government as potentially appropriate for Christians: from prayer to various kinds of activism, legal and illegal. He has endorsed lobbying, Christian political action committees, Christian Peacemaker Teams (he introduced the idea for CPTs at Mennonite World Conference in Strasbourg, France, in 1984), boycotts, civil disobedience, demonstrations, tax resistance, and noncooperation, claiming all can be consistent with Christian subjection to the divinely instituted authority of government.⁶⁰ In all these things Christians take the offensive in relation to the state, addressing it as a fallen power, called by God (through Christians' witness) to its rightful task of pursuing liberty, justice, and peace for all. Sider tends to identify God's agency with that

---

55 Sider, *Christ and Violence*, 59.
56 Sider, *Christ and Violence*, 59.
57 Sider, *Completely Pro-life*, 29.
58 Sider, *Completely Pro-life*, 29.
59 Sider, *Completely Pro-life*, 29.
60 See, for example, Sider, *Christ and Violence*, 60.

of the church at points: as God in Christ battled with the forces of evil, so "as the body of Christ, we are to continue the mission of the incarnate One in the world today and that includes an ongoing offensive against the fallen principalities and powers, a vigorous, active use of power in the search for greater justice in society."[61]

Concluding thoughts

Sider's position has many strengths. His emphasis on Christ's lordship over the world as well as the church is an important corrective to some traditional Mennonite preoccupation with Christ's lordship over the church alone. We are unavoidably and rightfully engaged with wider society. The shape of that involvement under the lordship of Christ is a crucial issue for Mennonites and Brethren in Christ in the late twentieth century.

Certainly, Sider is also right about the importance of wrestling with issues of power, coercion, violence, and nonviolence. We need to begin to make the kinds of distinctions he is struggling to form regarding right and wrong uses of power. And Sider and others are right to draw our attention to issues of justice too long neglected, to institutionalized evil and our participation in it, to our responsibility to address problems of injustice.

Sider also issues a vital challenge to us to become more faithful followers of Christ. It has become easy for North American Christians to offer glib advice to government regarding foreign and domestic policy, while we have lacked the will (or the Spirit) to put our own ecclesial houses in order. Sider is right to tell us that such counsel is fatuous as long as we are not taking the lead in our own communities of faith.

Some reservations remain for me about Sider's views. What are the biblical warrants for his high view of the state as an order of creation to serve the ends of liberty and justice? Is Sider's endorsement of democratic forms of government too uncritical? Are the twin goods of liberty and justice readily compatible? From a philosophical standpoint, the individual liberties Sider embraces are associated with philosophical liberalism's so-called "thin theory of the good" in which what is prized is governmental noninterference in freedom of expression, religion, family life, etc. How does this cohere with Sider's other norm for the state—that of justice, which he understands as substantial, and which needs a "thicker" understanding of the good, and a right of the state to interfere with people's

---

61 Sider, *Christ and Violence*, 58.

liberties (to exploit resources and accumulate wealth, for example) for the sake of correcting injustice?

I am uneasy, too, with Sider's apparent sense that God's primary concern with the movement of history is with what happens in government—with rulers, public policy, law. The church receives a significant share of Sider's attention, but sometimes its faithfulness seems to be important only as an instrument of wider social change. To overstate: the church should do God's will not because something of fundamental importance happens within the body, but because only then can its witness to the state have integrity and force. Ecclesiastical faithfulness seems to be important not in its own right but as a precondition of social transformation.

Sider's activist orientation sometimes also seems to confuse or conflate divine and human agency at points. Whose task is it to bring the rebellious powers in line with God's purposes? Sometimes that responsibility is assigned to God, and sometimes Sider's rhetoric seems to credit us with potentially world-changing opportunities for social involvement.

Sider's inattention to the question of duality of response (on the part of church and world) is also problematic. The acknowledgement of Christ's lordship and the enablement of the Holy Spirit surely make some difference. How should that difference be reflected in our witness to society and state?

Sometimes in his enthusiasm for the potential effectiveness of nonviolent techniques for accomplishing social change, Sider overlooks complications.[62] Where does the desire originate for the kind of just, peaceful society Sider holds up as a norm? What if people need to be recreated in order to long for that kind of society? Then Christians in North America cannot assume that the wider society shares our fundamental goals, and it is not just a question of whether nonviolent means are as effective as violent ones to attain them. Then the argument must address the issue of our being remade into a different sort of people with a desire for a different sort of society. The question of tactics is then a question of the tactics appropriate to the kind of people we are becoming.

How do we become people—hopeful, patient, courageous people—capable of sustained, nonviolent encounter with violence? How are we as Christians to be engaged with a wider society of people who do not share our longing for the kingdom, and who do not cultivate the virtues befitting people with such a hope? Certainly there will be some common

---

62 See especially Sider, *Non-Violence: The Invincible Weapon?*

ground, some opportunities to work together with nonbelievers and nonpacifist believers, but we are not helped to do so when we overlook the difference belief in a peaceable kingdom and a nonviolent Lord makes for our ethic.

Despite the optimistic tone of some of his utterances, Sider does confront us with the crucial reminder that peacemaking is difficult and risky business: if we are unwilling to prepare ourselves diligently, if we are unwilling to exercise our imaginations about nonviolent alternatives to violence, if we are unwilling to take risks to make peace—risks comparable to the risks assumed by those who make war—our peace witness is a relic, not a living force.

Type 7

Realist Pacifism

Lois Barrett

Duane Friesen, professor of Bible and religion at Bethel College (North Newton, Kansas), has advocated in his 1986 book a "Realist Pacifist" perspective on Christian peacemaking and international conflict.[1]

Summary

Separate roles for church and state

Friesen's peace theology assumes that the political organization of men and women is a good and necessary part of their creation as social beings. Political organization, including the nation-state, can be good or evil, because political power comes not primarily from the sword but from the consent of the governed. Friesen is not a naive optimist, however. He calls himself a realist because he "takes seriously the nature of human sinfulness as it expresses itself in the egoistic self-interest and exploitation of political and economic systems." But neither is he a pessimist, because he seeks to apply his pacifist ethic to "the resolution of practical, economic, and political issues within human institutions," particularly the nation-state (19). Christians and others become citizens of a nation-state involuntarily, by being born into it. But beyond national citizenship, Christians are to think of themselves as world citizens, caring for the peace and justice of the whole world. The nation-state is representative of the fallenness of politics in that no nation-state is universal, but claims only a specific geographic area.

The church, on the other hand, is a voluntary association; one chooses commitment to Christ. Although Friesen sometimes uses political language for the church, the church is not a political body, but a nongovernmental organization that takes Jesus as its norm (205). The church is "a new movement of people loyal to Christ [which] can create a powerful

---

[1] Duane K. Friesen, *Christian Peacemaking and International Conflict: A Realist Pacifist Perspective* (Scottdale, PA: Herald Press, 1986); all in-text citations are to this work.

liberating force for change in the midst of the principalities and powers" (91-92). The church "is a people of shalom which gathers regularly to discern their course of discipleship, and sustain their memory through corporate acts of worship—prayer, song, ritual. Then nourished and edified, they scatter to work for peace in a variety of capacities, some in organizations created specifically to promote peace, others in secular vocations to which they bring a peace perspective" (247).

This is not a two-kingdom theology in the strict sense, because although the church speaks to secular government and the claims of Christ take precedence over any claims of the nation-state, the church is not a government but a movement.

The relationship between church and state

The reason that Christians are involved in the political order of the nation-state is that God's salvation is not only individual and inward, but outward—political, social, and economic. "To restore the fundamental breach in relationship to God and in human relationships involves not only a change in inner attitude, but also a fundamental change in the structures that originally produced the damage and that continue to be perpetuated" (66). God, through the Bible, calls us to care about the oppressed. That care will happen not only through what the church does corporately, but through what Christians do to change the structures that oppress, including those of the nation-state.

Because those outside the church cannot be expected to have Jesus Christ as their norm, the church needs "middle axioms" in order to communicate with the secular world. Although the Christian faith involves relationship with God through Christ and an understanding of the story of Jesus, these middle axioms are principles that the secular world can understand. For Friesen, these principles are justice and nonviolence: justice as defined by Aristotle (to each his or her due), and nonviolence defined as not doing harm to or injuring people. Admittedly, this is a long way from love of enemies. "No direct application of theological-ethical norms to political reality can be made, since political institutions exist for quite different purposes than the church" (107). But the nation-state can be expected to serve its God-intended function of promoting the common good. One can urge the nation-state to take care of the downtrodden or to seek international arbitration rather than going to war. Thus, Friesen has a chapter that envisions a world in search of alternatives to military force as a way to solve international conflict. "That is utopian indeed, but so is the course [the superpowers] are now pursuing" (174).

Thus, there is really one ethic, one will of God for all people, in the church and out of the church. This ethic finds its most complete expression in the church, but it is translatable into secular language. God does not have one will for the church and another for the nation-state. Even though the nation-state will be able to go only so far in fulfilling that will outside of Christ, there is still one ethic, one goal for all people.

Christians' means of interaction with the state

The church contributes to justice first by its corporate way of life, and secondly in the way its members work within institutions, for social causes, and in influencing public policy. The church, as a worldwide pacifist community, promotes nonviolence within many societies, gradually undermining the various forms of legitimation of war, while developing new ways to handle international disputes (184-85). The church is to (1) help shape the character of society; (2) demonstrate justice and nonviolence in the church; (3) organize itself to meet human need in the world and thus provide models for others; (4) influence public policy, including voting; and (5) work as individuals in and through other institutions to further peace and justice (259).

Strategies for furthering peace and justice must be effective as well as faithful to Christian ethical principles. Although principles should never be violated for the sake of what works, an action is of little value if it accomplishes nothing. "One must calculate and carefully reason through the proposed action. Shouting in the streets to everyone in general but no one in particular may be legitimate, but it has little effectiveness in actually creating a peaceful world" (219). This should not exclude the witness of martyrdom, because "paradoxically, at times the only way to affirm life may be to accept death at the hand of a foe" (224). Friesen assumes that in many cases, though not all, nonviolent means can effectively further the cause of justice.

Toward an alternative politics for the church

A key assumption behind the realist pacifist position has to do with the nature of the church. Although this position sometimes uses biblical political language, in practice it follows the North American cultural assumption that the nation-state is a political body, but the church is a voluntary association, which works within the nation-state or perhaps across nation-state boundaries. The church itself is not a political body, except in the broadest sense of the word (it makes decisions, elects officers, etc.). This position usually understands separation of church and state to mean that church and state are different kinds of institutions, one political in essence, the other political only as it tries or its members try to influence government policies. The question of the relation between church and politics becomes: How do Christians—individually or corporately—influence what is happening in the real political arena, the nation-state?

Church and state as political bodies

What might this position look like if we regarded both the church (the holy nation) and the nation-state as political bodies? Both want to claim the Christian's allegiance. The church and the state differ not only in that the church claims Jesus as Lord, while the state puts ultimate trust in a human leader or constitution. They also differ in that they have different ways of defining citizenship and boundaries. The church's members are only those who have voluntarily covenanted with God and the church; the state includes as citizens everyone within certain geographical boundaries. Its membership is involuntary.

This geographical definition of the nation necessarily involves the sword as the ultimate sanction because the citizens of the state are not members by virtue of a voluntary commitment. There is a God-ordained function for the state: to work for the common good, and to keep order for all within its boundaries, non-Christian as well as Christian.

The people of Israel in their early history did not have geographical boundaries. In the wilderness this lack of boundaries is obvious. But even during the time of the judges, the geographical area of each tribe's influence included Canaanites and others not part of Israel. Not until the period of the kings did Israel attempt to claim all family groups within certain geographical boundaries as part of Israel.

In the New Testament, the church continued the tradition of early Israel, the holy nation, the people of God joined together by voluntary covenant. It was possible to trust God for defense, to take the long view of history, to function without the ultimate sanction of violence. The church is the way to be a political body without geographical boundaries and without a military. The church has its own legal system (see Matt. 18), its own defense (Eph. 6), its own pledge of allegiance, its own Lord.

Relationship of church and state

So how, then, does the church relate to the nation-state? By simply being the holy nation, the church witnesses to the lordship of Christ and to his way of peace. But beyond that, the nation-church relates to the nation-state by sending ambassadors. The Apostle Paul writes that Christ has commissioned us as ambassadors to carry the message of reconciliation to the world (2 Cor. 5:17-21). These ambassadors may practice diplomacy or may learn the languages of other nations, but the message is always that of inviting others to experience reconciliation and righteousness/justice/right relationships.

The diplomatic mission of the church to the state is similar to the mission of individual evangelism: calling people to repent, to commit their loyalties to God in Christ, and to follow Christ's way of loving enemies. Is it then worthwhile to proclaim that message to people or institutions that seem unlikely to repent?

We do well to regard church ethics and state ethics as on a continuum, rather than in two separate compartments. If this continuum is a vector pointing toward Christ (see fig. 7.1), then it is good to help anyone move along that vector closer to Christ. There is clearly a break in this continuum at the point of a decision to commit oneself to Christ and the church, but even before that commitment we can distinguish between worse and better behavior, decisions that lead one closer to the Christian way and decisions that take one in the opposite direction.

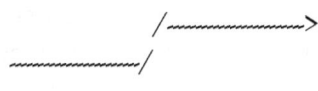

Figure 7.1

Thus, for example, the church can advocate that the state treat prisoners more humanely or decide not to build a new bomber—not because those actions are ultimately good, but because they move the state closer to the Christian way. This does not mean that the nation-state with its geographical, involuntary boundaries will ever become the holy nation. But that does not diminish the desirability of the church's sending its ambassadors with Christ's message.

Nonconformity and engagement with the powers

It is easiest for the church as holy nation, unconformed to the world, to withdraw from the world and try not to make waves. It is much more difficult to be different and stay connected, to keep proclaiming and doing reconciliation in the face of opposition, without running away or being co-opted. This is part of what it means to love enemies, to love those who are different from us: the church must remain engaged with the powers of the nation-state without withdrawing or being absorbed.

The social functions of realist pacifism

A further assumption of the "Realist Pacifism" position is that the church's social context is a relatively benevolent state, where there is some hope of influencing the actions of the state, and where Christians have comfortable niches within society, even though they may be a minority. Christians are a moral influence on society, the leaven in the loaf. The church exists to nurture and strengthen people for their vocation in the world.

This is in fact the way most North American Mennonite churches understand their context and accounts for the popularity of this variety of peace theology. But what if the state did not seem so benevolent? What if the church were less optimistic about its effectiveness in shaping the government's policies?

An alternative peace position in the New Testament is apocalypticism. Nonviolent apocalypticism has been an option for peoples through the centuries who are oppressed or relatively deprived of what they have had or have deserved. Deprived of hope that persecution will stop by human influence, apocalyptic looks to the future for God to step in and set things right. This is the position of the church in the Book of Revelation, where the state is the beast that Christ, the peaceful lamb who was slain, will conquer with the weapon of his mouth.

Whatever peace position Mennonite Central Committee advocates will make assumptions about the nature of the church and its social context. Should MCC adopt a position that reflects the situation of the majority of Mennonite congregations in North America? Or does a particular peace position that makes certain assumptions about the nature of the church and its context imply changes in our churches?

Analysis of "Realist Pacifism" following Burkholder's paradigm

T. Theological and biblical assumptions

T.1. The sovereignty of God

    T.1.a. God's ultimate will is shalom/wholeness for all people, although this is opposed now by the principalities and powers.

    T.1.b. God is active in history, intervening to restore human life to the original purposes for which God created it.

T.2. The lordship of Christ. Christ is Lord not only over the church, but over the principalities and powers, understood as social and political realities. Only the church, however, recognizes Christ as Lord and pattern for life.

T.3. Biblical interpretation

    T.3.a. Relation of Old and New Testaments. Both have social and political—rather than individualistic—content. We read the New Testament in the light of the Old Testament's concern for covenant, right relationships among people, justice, and liberation. The New Testament is the fulfillment of the Old. Jesus interprets his messiahship in terms of the suffering servant, rather than violent holy war.

    T.3.b. How does one derive ethical principles from Scripture? Our task as interpreters of the Bible is to try to discern the basic themes and perspectives on life reflected in the Bible. We must then seek to understand how these values apply to our new and different historical and cultural context.

    T.3.c. Functions and limits of hermeneutical community. The Spirit-guided community seeks to understand the meaning of the Bible in the community's social-political context. But our own cultural experience colors how we read the Bible.

T.4. Nature and scope of the gospel

    T.4.a. How are ethics and salvation related?

    T.4.b. In what sense is peace central to the gospel? Jesus's life and teachings are a continuation of the prophetic tradition, which emphasized justice, righteousness, and peace. Jesus's death on the cross is to be interpreted in the context of Jesus's life struggle to inaugurate the kingdom of righteousness. Jesus chose the role of the nonviolent servant to inaugurate his kingdom. Christ's servant role and acceptance of the cross is the most fundamental ethical model in the early church tradition. By his resurrection, Christ is Lord over the principalities and powers as well as the church, which is called to do battle with these powers by means of the gospel of peace. The new movement of people loyal to Christ can create a powerful liberating force for change in the midst of the principalities and powers.

T.5. Eschatology. Peace/shalom for the whole person and for the whole earth is the goal. The Christian is to live as if the future were already here and seek to translate that future into practical social and political action. The biblical image of a new heaven and a new earth gives a vision for social transformation within history.

E. Ethical principles and procedures

E.1. One morality? Yes, there is one ethic, one will of God for all people, in the church and outside the church, translatable into secular language. But Friesen recognizes that the nation-state will be able to go only so far in realizing that ethic.

E.2. Is it ever right to kill? No, but there should be a good coercion that "orders" human social behavior into patterns of cooperation. Persuasive force and coercive force may be necessary and acceptable if they are not violent, that is, if they do not harm people and if they initiate a process that can lead to reconciliation.

E.3. The Christian ethic is nonviolence rather than nonresistance.

E.4. Sources of ethical insight. Revelation is the source of ethical insight for people of faith, but it has to be translated into two mediating ethical concepts, justice and nonviolence, in order for Christians to cooperate with others in achieving larger political objectives. Biblical revelation is relational, coming to us through human experience.

E.5. Power and responsibility. Since political power rests in the consent of the governed, Christians, like others, have power to transform the world, and the responsibility to do so out of compassion for the world and because of their world citizenship.

C. The church

C.1. Relation of the kingdom of God and the visible church. The church is the institutional focus in history of the new ethical reality of the kingdom of God. Yet human visions and institutions are limited and imperfect expressions of the kingdom of God. The kingdom is future in the sense that God's rule is still coming in its fullness, but we can also expect the kingdom to break into our present history in a provisional way. Remnants thinking they represent the kingdom of God are warned against self-righteousness.

C.2. Priorities in mission. Speaking and acting on behalf of the poor and weak in the world is a priority. In the midst of the principalities and powers, the church should make its witness, both by bringing critical judgment on the powers' failure to serve human purposes, and by contributing creatively to the better structuring of social and cultural life. The church is to bring the good news of justice and peace to those in misery.

C.3. Social form and strategy. The church is a nongovernmental organization, a voluntary association, a people transcending national, racial, ethnic, ideological, and class lines, a force for change in the midst of the principalities and powers. The church is to provide spiritual resources for the vocation of peacemaking.

C.4. Tension of eternal and temporal dimensions of discipleship. The visible church is a fellowship of people bound by love who in eating the Lord's Supper together have a foretaste of the messianic banquet. The church demonstrates in the present what the future can be.

C.5. Decision-making processes. Discernment takes place in an atmosphere of mutuality, with dialogical give-and-take, culminating in consensus.

C.6. The church is a people of shalom gathering regularly to discern their course of discipleship and worship. Then nourished and edified, they scatter to work for peace in a variety of capacities.

S. The state and society

S.1. The nature of the state. The political organization of men and women (including the nation-state) is a good and necessary part of their creation as social beings.

S.2. Ethics of obedience/submission. The Christian position is neither total acceptance nor total rejection of the social structures. Sometimes Christians will not cooperate with institutions and may suffer for this. Civil disobedience is one of the ways to change social structures.

S.3. Citizenship.

> S.3.a. Christians are to think of themselves as world citizens, caring for the peace and justice of the whole world.

> S.3.b. Participation. Christians should not withdraw from but should participate in the transformation of social and cultural institutions. As beings made in the image of God the Creator, they are to become creators of culture. Christians are responsible to transform the political order.

S.4. State as guarantor of rights and freedoms. The God-intended function of the state is to serve the common good. All people are endowed with basic rights.

S.5. Legitimacy. Power comes not primarily from the sword or from the heads of state, but from the consent of the governed.

S.6. Sociocultural captivities and Christian discernment. Being Christian means having our views of justice shaped by the church rather than by the economic system in which we live.

S.7. Nature of international system. The international system is seen as a transnational network rather than in terms of a balance of power. A large number of actors—not just heads of state—affect the direction of international affairs.

S.8. Evaluation of ideologies and forms of government. Good government promotes peace and justice nonviolently and meets basic human needs. This position does not advocate capitalism, communism, or socialism as such.

P. Policies and positions on church-state issues

P.1. Patriotism and citizenship. Christians are world citizens first. The church extends beyond geographical boundaries.

P.2. Meaning of apolitical. Even withdrawal is a political stance. It may represent an alternative to the status quo, or, negatively, it may represent an attempt to escape from the world.

P.3. Magistracy. It is assumed that no particular candidate will be in full agreement with Christian ethical standards; the church can thus identify ethical criteria by which to assess candidates without endorsing any particular candidate. The question of whether Christians should run for public office is not addressed.

P.4. Appropriate witness to government authorities takes the form of helping shape the ethos of society and prepare people to accept nonviolent forms of conflict resolution aimed at a more just social structure; being an alternative society demonstrating nonviolence and justice; organizing service institutions to respond to human needs; organizing to shape public policy and to influence elected or appointed officials. Individual church members further peace and justice in and through the institutions where they work.

P.5. Criteria for evaluating public policies are the mediating principles of nonviolence and justice.

P.6. Strategy is also important. One should work toward effectiveness without sacrificing the principles of ethics. The means and the ends are connected.

D. Decisions on specific issues

D.1. Refusal to pay war taxes is a visible sign of an alternative way to live.

D.2. Draft resistance is a visible sign of an alternative way of living.

D.3. Laws on abortion. Not mentioned.

D.4. Foreign policy decisions should be made in conformity with the goals of peace and justice for all.

D.5. Cooperation with others working for peace and justice is commendable, even if they are working from a just war perspective.

D.6. International conflict can be solved by way of alternatives to military force.

D.7. Advocate human rights.

D.8. Help shape public policy against military spending and in favor of more social programs.

D.9. Help shape a third world development strategy that genuinely aids the poor.

D.10. Develop a model for a world order.

Type 8

A Perspective on Anabaptist Pacifism in Canada

John H. Redekop

Anabaptist sectarians' understanding of the state and their relationship to it should ideally not be influenced in fundamental ways by their particular social and political contexts. However, even a superficial examination of the experience of North American groups in the Anabaptist tradition (hereafter termed "Anabaptists") reveals substantial differences in outlook, which I believe are due in large part to their different Canadian and US national contexts. This brief essay attempts to explain, in a simplified way, why Anabaptist pacifism in Canada has become distinctive and, in particular, how and why it differs from the dominant expressions of Anabaptist pacifism in the United States. Anabaptists in Canada do not constitute a monolith; I will focus only on the dominant sectors.

Differences between Canadian and US Anabaptist pacifism

Three basic differences can be identified:

1. Canadian Anabaptists generally have a more positive view of the state and of government as an agent of the state. Much more than their US cousins, Canadians tend to see government as a servant and not mainly as a potential tyrant. They have difficulty perceiving government as an inherently evil enemy, an agency whose power is ultimately satanic, to paraphrase the Schleitheim confession of 1527. Canadian Anabaptists are therefore far less suspicious about government power and government money. They tend to view government as an agency established by God for the good of God's creation and generally hold it in high regard. On balance they see government in a positive light.

2. Canadian Anabaptists have readily entered into joint ventures with state authorities, including ventures that entail use of government funds. Though antipathy to war and rejection of military service apparently are no weaker in Canada than in the United States, at least according to data from World War

II, Anabaptist pacifists in Canada have been increasingly open to cooperative church-state ventures ranging from foreign aid to publication, and from victim-offender programs to the operation of many and varied institutions for needy people.[1] In partial contrast to the US experience, the traditional position of nonresistance has become politicized without becoming either ideological or largely negative. This development may be deemed either praiseworthy or lamentable.

MCC Canada's establishment of the Canadian Foodgrains Bank had the full support and cooperation of government agencies at various levels; Canadian Anabaptists saw this not as a risky compromise but as an authentic expression of their peace witness. Church, conference, and agency, including MCC Canada's, use of government funds to help people in need strikes most Canadian Anabaptists as a responsible and efficient utilization of their tax monies. They evidence little fear that they are selling out to Caesar or being manipulated by government for the government's advantage.

3. Canadian Anabaptists have moved broadly into political participation, including holding high elective offices and senior civil service posts; they have done so with extensive congregational approval. The history and extent of this involvement has been partially documented.[2]

The trend continues unabated. Typically, one or more Anabaptists can be found in the legislatures of each of the five western provinces, where 95 percent of Anabaptists reside, with several holding cabinet rank. Hundreds have run for provincial offices, in numerous cases several in one constituency. In several instances, all three or four candidates for a provincial seat were Anabaptists. Scores have run for seats in the national House of Commons, with approximately ten having been elected, all since 1945. At present, the Canadian House of Commons contains an

---

[1] See Guy Franklin Hershberger, *The Mennonite Church in the Second World War* (Scottdale, PA: Mennonite Publishing House, 1951), 34-48; John B. Toews, *A History of the Mennonite Brethren Church* (Hillsboro, KS: Mennonite Brethren Publishing House, 1975), 342-58.

[2] See John H. Redekop, "Mennonites and Politics in Canada and the United States," *Journal of Mennonite Studies* 1 (1983): 79-105.

Epp, a Friesen, a Funk, and a Reimer, with the Honorable Jake Epp serving as a prominent member of the national cabinet.

In the United States, according to available evidence, Anabaptists have been elected to Congress three times, all before 1938. In recent decades a few have run for office, but none has been elected. At the state level, perhaps ten have been elected, most before 1950. In general, Anabaptists do not have as high a profile in US politics as they do in Canadian politics. This difference reflects differences in grassroots values and theological priorities, as well as in demographics.

In Canada many Anabaptists see political involvement, in various political parties, as a positive witness within and to social structures, provided basic Anabaptist commitments are not undermined. Such attitudes seem less widespread in the United States. In the United States, Anabaptist political participation often appears to be done through Mennonite Central Committee, especially through its Peace Office and Washington Office. This different kind of involvement reflects and reinforces alternative expressions of activist Christian social concern. Canadian involvement is more positive in tone, US involvement more negative. Some observers see the US approach as more consistently critical and prophetic. Others see the Canadian as desirable because it utilizes opportunities more fully.

This survey of distinctive features of Canadian Anabaptist pacifism raises two key questions: Why did Canadian Anabaptist pacifism develop as it did? Does this pacifism have theological integrity?

Reasons for the development of a distinctive Anabaptist pacifism in Canada

Sociological factors

The Canadian and US migration patterns have been markedly different. According to 1990 data, almost three-quarters of the 266,100 Anabaptist church members in the United States are of Swiss Mennonite descent; in Canada only about one-eighth of the 114,400 church members are of the Swiss Mennonite group, almost all descended from immigrants from the United States. Because Anabaptists of Swiss descent have generally avoided political involvement, with some even refusing to vote, these different percentages have significant consequences. The fact that the Swiss Mennonite group has dominated the Anabaptist scene in the United States may well be the most important single factor shaping the kind of Anabaptist pacifism that has developed there.

The flip side of this picture involves the relative strength of the more politically active Dutch-Russian Mennonite group. While in the United States they constitute almost one-quarter of Anabaptists, in Canada the figure rises to almost seven-eighths.[3] The Dutch-Russian group brought to North America a tradition of extensive political interaction, first with the Czarist regime and then, for the large numbers who came in the 1920s and 1940s, with Soviet authorities. The Dutch-Russian group had also had extensive political experience in governing their own colonies.

It is significant, too, that though the first wave of Anabaptist immigrants from Russia, in the 1870s, settled almost exclusively in rural areas, those who came after 1920 settled largely in urban centers. In the United States there were no major immigrations after the world wars, and therefore even among the Dutch-Russian group the earlier rural orientation and settlement patterns remained dominant. The Swiss group, with settlements in Pennsylvania as early as 1683, remained almost entirely rural, pursuing mainly agricultural and related vocational trades and generally shunning political affairs. Their minimal political acculturation before the twentieth century and their broad rejection of political involvement have shaped the general direction of Anabaptist pacifism in the United States. In Canada, on the other hand, Dutch-Russian immigrants after World Wars I and II soon achieved educational, vocational, and financial success, and many became politically active.

In the United States, Anabaptists are more numerous than in Canada, but are less significant numerically. Approximately one of every 900 people in the United States is an Anabaptist; in Canada this ratio is one in 230. Moreover, in Canada most Anabaptists are concentrated in several regions and cities where they form a significant voting bloc. In some towns and rural areas, they constitute a majority and determine electoral and policy matters. Even in some large urban areas they form a significant minority. Winnipeg, for example, has a population of about 585,000; the 47 Anabaptist congregations there have about 20,000 members, and perhaps another 15,000–20,000 are children, or adults who do not belong to a church.[4] In the United States, on the other hand, where there are concentrations of Mennonite and Amish people, as in parts of Pennsylvania, many have chosen not to become involved politically.

---

3 Rodney J. Sawatzky, "Domesticated Sectarianism: Mennonites in the U.S. and Canada," *Canadian Journal of Sociology* 3, no. 2 (1978): 240; Dieter Goetz Lichdi, *Mennonite World Handbook* (Carol Stream, IL: Mennonite World Conference, 1990), 328.

4 Leo Driedger, *Mennonites in Winnipeg* (Winnipeg: Kindred Press, 1990), 87.

Historical factors

Canadian Anabaptists, whether Amish, Mennonite, or Brethren in Christ, did not come to a country the founders of which had revolted against political exploitation and oppression. The political climate they encountered did not include fear of government. In fact, in most cases the Canadian government actually functioned as the agent that made migration to Canada a possibility for these people. The British colonial authorities and, after 1867, the Canadian government served to welcome the United Empire Loyalists, including Anabaptists fleeing America's Revolutionary War in the 1780s, the Dutch-Russian immigrants in the 1870s, and also the Dutch-Russian displaced persons who arrived after both world wars. Many Anabaptist immigrants to Canada in the twentieth century were particularly grateful to the Canadian government for welcoming them at a time when other governments, including that of the United States, had generally refused entry to them.

Since early colonial days, relations between church and state in Canada have been amicable, with religious and governmental bodies cooperating outright in public education and many other areas. Canada has no legacy of a presumed "wall of separation" between church and state. In fact, for millions of Catholic French Canadians, as well as people representing other smaller cultural groups (Italian Catholics, Scottish Presbyterians, Swedish Lutherans, Dutch Reformed people, Mennonites), the notion of a mosaic of ethnic faith-groups cooperating with government while retaining their identity and peculiarity was central to their understanding of life in the Dominion. To this day ethnic Mennonites, Dukhobors, Hutterites, and many other ethno-religious groups interact comfortably with provincial and national governments in a host of matters.

Further, throughout Canadian history, and especially since Canada's formal founding in 1867, church-state controversies have been few. More often than not government has functioned as a friend of the church. Canadian authorities have not only strongly supported Christianity in the school systems, but they have also promoted Christian holy days, encouraged public prayer anywhere, at least until the entrenchment of the Charter of Rights and Freedoms in 1982, and have granted a variety of faith groups special exemptions and privileges. In recent years, governments have also worked with religious groups to provide services to Native peoples, to provide overseas relief, to sponsor refugees, and to pursue other cooperative projects of mutual interest.

Given such experiences, why should Canadian Anabaptists view government as suspect or evil? Of course, there have been evil tendencies in government, and some disgusting abuses of power, but the extent of the evil seems no greater than that found in business, labor, or any other segment of a sub-Christian society.

Not surprisingly, then, most Canadian Anabaptists have quickly developed deep gratitude for the freedoms and goodwill extended to them by government and have thanked God for a land where they could, by and large, go about their pacifist way of life unhindered. For cooperative projects and for special privileges they have been doubly grateful.

The general religious scene

Although Christianity, at first mainly Catholic and Anglican, has enjoyed an honored place in Canadian history, it has not become politicized the way it has in the United States. Conservative Christianity has not become fused with conservative politics, nor has liberal Christianity become fused with liberal politics. No sector of the Christian community has merged its faith with patriotism to any significant extent. Canada has experienced nothing analogous to the development of Christian-Americanism. There is no concept of Christian-Canadianism, and no Canadian equivalent of American "Manifest Destiny." Canadian Anabaptists, and Canadian Christians in general, have not faced a sentimental, state-related religiosity or the cultic assumptions underpinning such entities. Civil religion has never thrived in Canada. No pledge of allegiance here includes "under God"; in fact, Canadians have no pledge of allegiance at all. "In God We Trust" has never been a national motto. In short, though Canadian Anabaptists have often had good reason to be critical of their government, they have not had to deal with a state that claims a divine mission or some special mandate under God.

Two other religious factors should be noted. First, the percentage of evangelicals in Canada has for generations been less than a third of that in the United States, and they have not sought or possessed political clout. Canada has had no Moral Majority, no televangelists playing chaplain to the country and its leaders, no religious Far Right of any consequence. Because this is so, Canadian Anabaptists have been able to express their conservative religious concerns to government without having to differentiate themselves from passionate Christian defenders of the political establishment or from extremists wishing to use the law to achieve their political utopia or to suppress their critics. The absence, for better or worse, of political-religious quarrels about what Canada was at the time of its founding, or about what Canada is destined to be, has facilitated reasoned Anabaptist communication with the state and has prevented the development of overly critical attitudes about what the state has claimed or done.

Political factors

Significantly, Canadians have never seen the slowly developing and still incomplete Canadian constitution as in any way divinely inspired, nor have they assumed the country's symbols to be sacred. This is true despite the fact that the monarch, the formal head of state, also bears the title "Defender of the Faith." Canadian political arrangements are not seen as better than those of other countries, let alone particularly moral, ideological, or ultimate. They are perceived instead as pragmatic and utilitarian. Canadian founders are not revered as saints (no holidays are devoted to any of them), national buildings are not shrines, and national political holidays have virtually no religious content. When a state does not set itself up as a religious entity, Anabaptists have less reason to react negatively to it.

Accordingly, when Canadian Anabaptists dialogue and even cooperate with the state, they are not dealing with a power demanding ultimate allegiance; the state does not challenge the primacy of Christians' allegiance to the church. The Canadian state expresses its claims almost entirely in strictly political rather than in political-moral terms. Consequently, dealings with government do not begin in a framework of competing or threatening claims. Because the Canadian state structure has little ideological content, Canadian Anabaptists have not felt threatened, and have actually had broad opportunities for involvement in state decision-making.

Canadian citizenship gives one political and cultural rather than moral or ideological identity. Canadians do not regard the state as given; they do not have to struggle to reconcile the ultimately irreconcilable beliefs that (1) their state is uniquely sanctioned by God, and (2) it is potentially tyrannical. Because most Canadian Anabaptists hold neither view, they do not wrestle with these divergent beliefs.

Canadian nationalism deserves notice. It is so weak a force that Canadians watched quietly in 1980 when the Province of Quebec conducted a referendum to decide whether it would leave Canada. By a 59.6 percent vote, Quebec decided to stay. Again in 1990 Canadians watched with interest but without anxiety or dismay as Quebec threatened to leave the federation.

Such weak nationalism, perhaps a mark of political rationality and maturity, is both functional and dysfunctional. Canada may lack the commitment, the glue, to hold together. But this very weakness is good in the sense that Christians, including Anabaptists, are not subjected to powerful political pressures, and are not tempted to see national political structures as the framework within which all else makes sense. Nationalism has not become a divisive force in the church; political ventures have not become crusades.

Despite the weakness of Canadian nationalism, Canadians in general agree that the Canadian state, though fragile, exists for an important but not unique or divinely ordained purpose. That role is to restrict evil and be a servant for good. Government apparatus may expand substantially to facilitate public action to achieve public good. Because Canadians lack reasons to be suspicious of government, they generally react positively when state structures undertake regulatory, welfare, and even proprietary ventures. Canadian socialism, rooted more in Methodism than in Marx, is viewed as a legitimate part of the ideological landscape; this contrasts with prevailing US views of socialism. Therefore, Canadians do not mind when government undertakes an array of socialistic programs ranging from public hospital and medical insurance to family allowances. Some Anabaptists have even suggested that such ventures incorporate elements of the Christian ethic. Other Anabaptists, particularly those who remember—or remember hearing about—the socialist policies of Soviet communism, disagree.

In any event, most Canadians think their government serves them well by using for social programs a large part of the money it raises from them via taxation. This broad acceptance of government as economic leveler and provider, entrepreneur and regulator, has given rise to Canada's "public enterprise culture." Even Canadians, including Canadian Anabaptists, who vote for political parties supporting more free enterprise tend to see government as a helpful though inefficient service agency needed to help those who cannot help themselves. They view government as God-given, entrusted with the positive task of assisting marginalized people.[5]

---

5 See John H. Redekop, "The State and the Free Church," in *Kingdom, Cross, and Community: Essays on Mennonite Themes in Honor of Guy F. Hershberger*, edited by John Richard Burkholder and Calvin Redekop (Scottdale, PA: Herald Press, 1976), 179-95.

Several additional political factors deserve mention here. First, Canada is a middle power playing no major military role on the world stage. It has decided not to develop a nuclear arsenal or even a substantial conventional military force. Though it has the seventh-largest economy in the western world and has been the country most extensively used in United Nations peacekeeping efforts, Canada has only a small military budget, about nine percent of total government expenditure. The comparable US figure is near 40 percent. Criticizing military spending and the military-industrial complex therefore has a different hue in Canada than in the United States.

Since the Korean "police action" of the early 1950s, Canada has not been involved in any war. It has had no draft since World War II. It did not experience the wrenching impact of the Vietnam War. In fact, in Indochina and elsewhere Canada has served as a peacekeeper rather than a combatant. But Canada does manufacture and export many weapons. Many Canadian Christians, including Anabaptists involved in Project Ploughshares, Mennonite Central Committee, and other agencies, continue to remind the Canadian government and munitions makers that foreign aid should take other forms.

Second, Canadians note with satisfaction that many of the government's broad, generous social programs were humanitarian ventures first pioneered by the churches. Health care, education from kindergarten to university, help for the disabled, homes for the elderly, assistance for the destitute, and many other projects upholding human dignity fall into this category. Foreign aid is yet another example. Small wonder that Canadian Anabaptists and other Christians affirm these government programs and are pleased that the state takes over projects the church first modeled.

General observations

In part because of the nature of the Canadian state, and in part because of their mainly positive experiences with it, Canadian Anabaptists have few negative attitudes toward their state. Why should they? One can of course identify policy shortcomings, but these suggest short-term political opportunism rather than a deep, intrinsic propensity for evil.

Apart from some wartime difficulties, Canadian Anabaptists have generally had good relations with government in dealings about land grants, separate schools, language rights, alternatives to military service, family unification, government funding for care homes and senior citizen residences, immigration matters, victim-offender reconciliation programs, distribution of surplus government commodities, work with Native peoples, and overseas relief and development grants. This broad spectrum of positive interaction has had a major impact on attitudes. In sum, most Canadian Anabaptists have overcome some earlier reluctance about government assistance and their own interaction with government and now see the state in a positive light.

In recent decades Anabaptists in the United States have also become more active politically than they had been. But they have played a smaller role than in Canada, partly because of their smaller numbers relative to their larger society, partly because of the views of the dominant Swiss segment, partly because of the different priorities of the US government, and partly because they have held closer to traditional Anabaptist theological norms about avoiding politics. Perhaps the still-dominant rural mindset and lack of immigrants during the past sixty years have also played a part. In any event, as Anabaptists in the United States try to sort out their complex church-state issues, and they have done vastly more research and writing in this area than have Canadians, they struggle to reconcile their generally positive experiences of the state and their generally negative theology of the state.

In sum, it seems accurate to say that most Canadian Anabaptists have come to view government as simply another arena in which they should participate to the extent that Christian servanthood permits, and that most US Anabaptists view the political order as outside God's mandate for Christian participation. No doubt, both groups can learn from each other, as they agree that Christian political involvement must always be conditional, always secondary, always alert and prophetic.

Conclusion

1. Though Canadian and US Anabaptists manifest no basic differences in theological assumptions about church-state relations, they have had substantially different experiences with their governments and face markedly different political situations in the two countries.

2. Governments in both countries have positive and negative dimensions. Anabaptist peace witness in each country is influenced by which aspects are selected for analysis and emphasis.

3. By and large, US Anabaptists, especially those less educated, have a stronger nationalistic commitment, but are less active

in politics. Conversely, Canadian Anabaptists appear to be less nationalistic but more active politically, especially in partisan electoral pursuits and in joint ventures.

4. Although the US Constitution makes much of a wall of separation between church and state, in practice religion and politics have been at least as intermingled in the United States as in Canada. One big difference is that in the United States the courts have for generations defined many problem areas. With the entrenchment of the Charter of Rights and Freedoms in Canada in 1982, Canadians are beginning to see similar trends. As the courts become more active in church-state issues, Canadian Anabaptists will find themselves involved in more disputes.

5. Most US Anabaptists have strong suspicions about government power and money. Their Canadian counterparts tend not to. Having absorbed much of their country's public enterprise culture and their society's positive view of government, they gladly accept government grants, which they see as putting their own tax money to good use. Thus, Canadian Anabaptists, much more than Anabaptists in the United States, tend to see cooperation with government as acceptable, even desirable.

6. Although most US Anabaptists have been more reluctant than Canadian Anabaptists to jump into the political arena, they have led the way in study and writing about church-state issues.

7. Canadian Anabaptists can help their brothers and sisters in the United States by criticizing US civil religion, the idea of the United States's uniqueness, Christian-Americanism, and a preoccupation with the negative dimensions of government. US Anabaptists can help their Canadian sisters and brothers by criticizing Canadian political self-righteousness, their sometimes uncritical political activism, and their preoccupation with the positive dimensions of the state. Each group must learn to view church-state relations from the perspective of the other. Canadian Anabaptists are too sanguine, too confidently optimistic, too anti-American. Canadian Anabaptists are more satisfied with their experiences as Canadian citizens than they should be. US Anabaptists tend to be too selective in their assessment of US policies, too ready to believe damning reports, and too hesi-

tant to believe positive reports about their government's activities. They have allowed too much distance to develop between Washington MCC staff and congregational grassroots.

8. The spiritual kinship between Anabaptists in Canada and the United States remains strong. That kinship should be nurtured and used to counteract the divisive effects of living in notably different church-state settings. Many misunderstandings about church-state matters will recede as the two communities reevaluate their basic stances and listen to one another. Our common identity and calling facilitate mutual understanding. But the task of building greater unity is complicated by the fact that both groups' theology and practice have been shaped by their respective societies more than they realize.

9. The Christian church is called to an ethic of discipleship, based on love. Government is called to an ethic of justice and to facilitating individual and group fulfillment. Both Canadian and US Anabaptist communities are grateful for the privilege of living in societies committed to freedom and where opportunities for Christian service abound. Both groups realize that political irrelevance is not an option. Both know they must take politics seriously without giving it the status of ultimate seriousness. And both acknowledge that ability plus opportunity equals accountability.

Type 9

Liberation Pacifism

Robert J. Suderman

In his preliminary essay that shaped the agenda for this symposium, John R. Burkholder sketched a provisional typology of Mennonite peace theologies. He suggested three characteristics of the liberation pacifism type (1) it begins by standing in solidarity with the poor and oppressed; (2) it emphasizes justice, perhaps treating justice as more primary than peace; (3) it is reluctant to establish absolute nonviolence as a norm. Arnold Snyder, Perry Yoder, Mark Neufeld, and perhaps LaVerne Rutschman were noted as possible examples of this type.

Do these characteristics really identify this literature? The first theme cited is not limited to this type. Most Mennonite theology attempts to demonstrate solidarity with the poor, although this is not always the starting point. The second characteristic needs further definition. The question of the relative priority given to justice and peace, or whether in fact the two can be separated and thus ranked at all, is an issue that is not limited to this type either.

It is the third characteristic that specifically interests us. Are Snyder, Neufeld, Yoder, and Rutschman reluctant to see nonviolence as a norm in all situations? If so, what are the reasons for this reluctance? What alternatives do they suggest? How would this affect our mission strategy and peace witness? With these questions in mind, we turn to the articles by Snyder and Neufeld.

Summary

Mark Neufeld

Mark Neufeld, in his article "Critical Theory and Christian Service: Knowledge and Action in Situations of Social Conflict," bases his analysis of appropriate action and knowledge on the critical social theory of

Jürgen Habermas.[1] Integral to all human development are three types of knowledge: technical, hermeneutic, and critical. Each type of knowledge responds to special interests of the community.

"Technical knowledge" is geared toward "transforming the physical environment" for human survival (250). Because Christian service is interested in more than physical survival, this knowledge is necessary but not adequate for Christian service. The danger comes in extending "the technical view of knowledge to the social world" (251). This results in use of social engineering techniques: treating people as objects and manipulating them for predetermined goals; defining social peace in terms of maintaining order; supporting institutions concerned with restoring order; giving primary attention to the interests of the elite, with little attention devoted to root problems that affect the majority poor.

"Hermeneutic knowledge" is interested in social communication for purposes of understanding the social order. Both communication and understanding are defined in "nonpolitical" and "nonideological" terms (254). Hermeneutic knowledge views social breakdown in terms of "miscommunication and misperception" (255). Thus, conflict mediation/resolution is the appropriate technique for resolving social tensions. Neufeld indicates that the main weakness of this approach is that it "provides no means for identifying . . . ideological distortions, no criteria for critically assessing competing interpretive frameworks" (256). This mediation/resolution approach also does not provide criteria with which to understand structurally generated social conflict, and thus cannot get at the roots of social conflict. Neufeld asserts that "reform-minded North American liberals," including liberal Mennonites and Mennonite Central Committee, base their attempts at social reform on these assumptions (254-55).

"Critical knowledge" is interested in emancipation "from structurally generated distortions of human interaction" (257). Its tools are the critical social sciences, and its purpose is critique. "What the critical social sciences all share is the premise that distortions in human interaction are rooted in socially structured inequalities (e.g., of wealth and power). Because inequalities are seen to be socially structured—and not as part of a pre-given natural order—they can be overcome" (258). This approach thus provides what the hermeneutic approach did not: criteria for assessing, "in an open, nondogmatic and critical manner," competing interpreta-

---

[1] Mark Neufeld, "Critical Theory and Christian Service: Knowledge and Action in Situations of Conflict," *Conrad Grebel Review* 6, no. 3 (1988): 249-62; in-text citations in sections on Neufeld are to this article.

tions of social reality (258). Those interpretations that develop critical social understandings and empower people to struggle for justice are considered superior.

The approach is realistic about the nature of social interaction; it recognizes that social conflict cannot always be "'harmonized'" through understanding and mediation. Sometimes resolution only comes by structural transformation, by revolutionary organized struggle (259). The advantage of this model for Christian service is that it coincides with the heart of the Christian gospel, i.e., salvation, liberation, emancipation from sin. "Here, peacemaking is conceived not as enforcing order nor as 'helpful' impartial mediation, but rather as participating in a struggle for social justice; not as manipulating the oppressed, nor even standing with and listening to the oppressed, but as working alongside the oppressed for radical social change" (260). Neufeld exhorts Christian service organizations, including MCC, to adopt this emancipatory approach even if it means losing some constituency support.

Arnold Snyder

In "The Relevance of Anabaptist Nonviolence for Nicaragua Today," Arnold Snyder compares the Peasants' War in the early sixteenth century with the Nicaraguan Revolution of 1979.[2] He notes that in response to the peasant upheaval, Anabaptists at Schleitheim in 1527 "rejected armed resistance and called for a nonviolent response" (112). Snyder's intent is to explore whether this call to nonviolence is still relevant in a modern setting such as the Nicaraguan Revolution. "Since the Anabaptist nonviolent tradition is revolutionary in origin, does it have anything relevant to say to Christians actively involved in revolutions today? Is Anabaptist nonviolence a step forward toward justice, peace and love, or a step backward toward oppression, exploitation and grief?" (115).

Snyder describes how the German peasants' (and Nicaraguans') concerns for justice "eventually led some Christians to attack the agents of injustice with counter-violence" (117). He suggests that the revolutionaries and the Schleitheim Anabaptists had significantly different views of Christ. For the revolutionaries, "self-sacrificing actions that lead to greater justice for the people as a whole are Christlike actions" (119); this justifies

---

[2] C. Arnold Snyder, "The Relevance of Anabaptist Nonviolence for Nicaragua Today," in *Freedom and Discipleship*, edited by Daniel S. Schipani (Maryknoll, NY: Orbis Books, [1984] 1989), 112-27 (reprinted from *The Conrad Grebel Review* 2, no. 2 [Spring 1984]: 123-37); in-text citations in sections on Snyder are to this essay.

active participation in revolution. For the Schleitheim Anabaptists the submissive and spiritual Christ, who suffered rather than retaliate, is the model of obedience to be followed. For them, "the fullness of the kingdom must await Christ's return" (119).

Snyder suggests that "the Achilles heel of the Schleitheim position of nonviolence is its lack of concern with matters of justice in the wider world. Rather than teaching an ethic of justice, it preaches an otherworldly ethic of purity and holiness in expectation of Christ's imminent return" (120). On the other hand, "the Achilles heel of the liberation justification of violence is the appeal to the incarnate Christ as example." Jesus' life does not provide us with "a convincing example of revolutionary violence" (121).

Is nonviolence relevant to a modern revolutionary context? Snyder suggests that "passive," "escapist," "separatist," "eschatological," "boring," "complacent," "quiet," "dualist," and "silent" nonviolence (the Schleitheim variety) "will not be relevant to our Nicaraguan brothers and sisters, regardless of how fine and correct our conception of Christ may be" (122). On the other hand, nonviolence that is "active," "confrontational," committed to "direct action" to prevent "the violence of injustice, starvation, disease and murder" (122), and "fearlessly engaged" in the struggle for justice in the world, "this is a nonviolence that is relevant to Nicaragua and to all the world, and it is relevant because it actively teaches and demonstrates a committed, nonviolent concern for the welfare of our neighbor in need" (122).

Nonviolence was never part of the process of evangelization in Nicaragua, and therefore, in the words of Miguel d'Escoto, "We have no right to hope to harvest what we have not sown'" (122). We will sow the seeds of nonviolence by example or not at all. Thus, the only Anabaptist vision worthy of recovery "is the totally engaged Anabaptism that dies to self only to rise fearlessly in Christ. Such discipleship will not shrink from acting on behalf of the powerless and violated, as we know Christ himself did when he was among us" (122).

Analysis

Mark Neufeld

Mark Neufeld's thesis is attractive to modern Anabaptists. It goes beyond transforming the physical environment, beyond impartial friendliness, to a radical concern for restructuring the social system to enable the poor and oppressed to benefit from its blessings. This position is eager to take a stand and suggests limited criteria to guide our choosing sides. The social science perspective illuminates the structural face of evil, and is a welcome corrective to modern individualistic piety. This view also correctly sees that emancipation in all its dimensions is at the heart of the gospel.

Contrary to Neufeld's assessment of MCC, however, I would suggest that Habermas's three types of knowledge appear to correspond with MCC's historical trajectory: (1) involvement in relief work (technical knowledge); (2) participation in development (hermeneutic knowledge); and (3) concern for justice (critical knowledge).

Some additional points need to be tested. Is this social science premise—that distortions in human interaction are rooted not in a pre-given natural order but in socially structured inequalities, and therefore can be overcome—an adequate basis for Christian service? Is this not a sophisticated restatement of the nineteenth-century liberal optimism that Neufeld himself wants to discredit? Neufeld believes that this time the critical social sciences can search for truth in an open, nondogmatic, critical manner (258). Is this faith in the social sciences warranted? Do these sciences not have their own presuppositions which determine the route that "critical analysis" will take?

How would the proposed criteria of the social sciences (i.e., does it elucidate? does it empower?) result in resolution in the case of the competing interpretive frameworks of the Filipino fishermen Neufeld mentions (256, n. 23)? One poor fisherman blamed problems on Filipino Muslims, another on rich Filipinos who exploit the poor. Perhaps stoning all Muslims (as the first fisherman proposed) would empower the fishermen of his island.

Is Neufeld's conviction that all evil (distortion) is contained in social structures an adequate understanding of the biblical concept of the fall?

Is Neufeld reluctant to establish absolute nonviolence as a norm, as John R. Burkholder suggests? Neufeld repeatedly fails to define the word that could shed light on that question. He suggests that "structural change requires struggle which is, by definition, revolutionary" (259); transformation of social structures can come only through "organized struggle" (260); peacemaking means "participating in a struggle for social justice" (260); Christian service workers must understand that societal transformation comes "through struggle" (260); and Christian service should involve "joining with the poor to . . . organize for a more effective struggle" (261). His critique of MCC implies that its present strategies prevent

MCC workers from participating in this struggle, but nowhere does he define its nature. Does he advocate violence as part of the struggle for justice in MCC's programs? Is he reluctant to establish nonviolence as a norm? Does he fit Burkholder's characterization of this type? These questions go unanswered.

Arnold Snyder

Snyder's position is easier to isolate. An unfaithful or disobedient type of nonviolence must never be held up as a norm by Anabaptist Christians. Such nonviolence "will not be relevant, for we are speaking mere words rather than acting to prevent the violence suffered by our brothers and sisters" (122). On the other hand, an active nonviolence, faithful and obedient to Jesus (as Snyder understands him), is normative for Anabaptists and others. "This is a nonviolence that is relevant to Nicaragua and to all the world, and it is relevant because it actively teaches and demonstrates a committed, nonviolent concern with the welfare of our neighbor in need" (122). Snyder is not reluctant to establish the right kind of nonviolence as a norm.

Three points in Snyder's paper deserve closer attention from Mennonite historians more qualified than I am to test them.

First, is Snyder's characterization of Schleitheim accurate? If so, should this type of nonviolence be considered apostasy in modern revolutionary contexts?

Second, Snyder claims that the Anabaptist nonviolent tradition is "post-revolutionary in origin" (115). Is this accurate? Did Anabaptists opt for nonviolence because of persecution they experienced in a revolutionary setting (making their nonviolence post-revolutionary), or were they persecuted in part because they opted for nonviolence (making nonviolence part of the revolutionary struggle and strategy)? Was Schleitheim the beginning of the process of conceptualizing and applying nonviolence to a concrete situation, or was it the solidification of a process that had begun well before Schleitheim (and perhaps even before the Peasants' War)? If in fact the Anabaptist tradition of nonviolence was formulated before or in the midst of revolutionary times, as Conrad Grebel's letters to Thomas Müntzer seem to suggest,[3] then Snyder's position should be reevaluated.

---

3 Leland Harder, ed., *The Sources of Swiss Anabaptism: The Grebel Letters and Related Documents* (Scottdale, PA: Herald Press, 1985); see especially 290, 293.

Third, Snyder characterizes Schleitheim nonviolence as follows:

> When we imagine applying the separatist, eschatological and passive nonviolence of Schleitheim to such a situation [i.e., Nicaragua, where Christians paid in blood to overthrow their dictator], I fear that we must say that such passive nonviolence would result in an increase in oppression and exploitation. In fact, what imperialist power would not sincerely encourage all of its colonists to believe in passive nonviolence of this kind? They would be obedient and quiet subjects, a little on the boring side, to be sure, but certainly not people to worry about. Generations would come and go, concerned only with giving a passive witness, waiting patiently for divine justice to descend from heaven. Machiavelli in his wildest dreams could not have devised a better formula. (120)

The sixteenth-century experience does not seem to support Snyder's fear. There is every indication that the powers worried a great deal about these "quiet," "boring" people. Is Snyder suggesting that this concern was due only to other factors (baptizing adults, challenging church doctrine, establishing communities)? The sixteenth-century Anabaptists even after Schleitheim were not treated as Machiavelli's dream children by the Machiavellis of the time. Still, one cannot accuse Snyder of reluctance in applying nonviolence as a norm.

Historians may challenge his interpretation of history, and exegetes may challenge his reading of Jesus, but within his own exegetical and historical framework Snyder strongly affirms both nonviolence as a revolutionary strategy, and obedience to Jesus, the Lord of history.

Liberation pacifism

It may be fruitful to spend a moment with liberationist thought that could truly be characterized as reluctant to establish absolute nonviolence as a norm. In his essay, "On Discipleship, Justice and Power," Míguez Bonino states:

> Force, including physical compulsion and violence in its many forms, is part of that [secular or structural] realm [in which all humanity is included and where all will function according to the nature of that realm]. We cannot

will it out of existence. But some Christians and Christian communities—and I feel personally drawn in that direction—have consistently refused to accept this mode of participation. . . . We can be pacifists! When this decision is taken in the context of a Christian witness that includes responsibility for the realm of the world, I find it legitimate.[4]

Míguez Bonino's temptation toward pacifism is tempered by several factors, however: (1) pacifism need not be considered the compulsory option for all Christians; (2) we cannot invoke the example of Jesus by "mere transposition"; and (3) we must "conform to 'the form of existence of Jesus' at a deeper level."[5] Whether this deeper level of conformity includes the possibility of the use of violence "seems to me still an open theological (and existential) question to which there cannot be ready-made answers."[6] Míguez Bonino appears to be a pacifist who is reluctant to establish nonviolence as an absolute norm. He fits Burkholder's type.[7]

George V. Pixley's "Response from a Baptist Biblical Scholar" also seems to fit this type.[8] He speaks about the dilemma of a Christian pacifist community (the Mennonites) living in the wealthiest nation in the world, which is threatening the freedom Nicaraguans have achieved. He suggests two alternatives: (1) emigration, or (2) "a radical evangelical questioning of Anabaptism as a form of Fundamentalism."[9] Then he states: "My own way to solve the dilemma would be simply to take nonviolence as a recommended but not an absolute value of the kingdom. But I am a Baptist and this is not my problem."[10]

Juan Luis Segundo is more emphatic in his rejection of nonviolence as a norm for Christian conduct. He attempts to separate faith from ideology: faith is absolute, but empty of specific content; ideology has con-

---

4 José Míguez Bonino, "On Discipleship, Justice and Power," in *Freedom and Discipleship*, edited Daniel S. Schipani (Maryknoll, NY: Orbis Books, 1989), 137-38.

5 Míguez Bonino, "On Discipleship, Justice and Power," 138.

6 Míguez Bonino, "On Discipleship, Justice and Power," 138.

7 For more details of Míguez Bonino's arguments, see José Míguez Bonino, *La fe en busca de eficacia* (Salamanca, Spain: Ediciones Sigueme, 1977), chap. 6.

8 George V. Pixley, "Response from a Baptist Biblical Scholar," in *Freedom and Discipleship*, 139-46.

9 Pixley, "Response from a Baptist Biblical Scholar," 145.

10 Pixley, "Response from a Baptist Biblical Scholar," 145.

tent but does not represent "any objectively absolute value."[11] Historical experience is ideological, and therefore no ethical approach is absolute. The void between absolute faith and historical options must be filled with ideology. The extermination of enemies in the Old Testament and nonresistant love in the New Testament are both attempts to fill this void. These are examples of "ideology, not . . . the content of faith."[12] The absolute quality of the Christian faith does not lie in its content but in its "liberative process. It is converted into freedom for history, which means freedom for ideologies."[13]

On the basis of his exegesis of the New Testament documents, Segundo affirms that Jesus was a nonviolent agitator who commanded mutual and suffering love. Using the parable of the Good Samaritan, however, he points to five factors that lead him away from an absolute pacifist position:[14]

1. The tools of love and the tools of violence are in fact the same. By choosing to "love" the man in the ditch, the Samaritan chose to do "violence" to others who were also in the ditch.

2. Because of the limitations of historicity, our "economy of energy" forces us to choose whom we love (give our time and energy to). This choice does violence to those we do not choose.

3. Historical efficacy forces us to choose prudently where and how our economy of energy will be directed.

4. "All the remarks we find in the Bible about violence and nonviolence are ideologies," and all ideologies are relative.[15] None can be taken as absolute ethical norms.

5. The end must always justify the means. A means "cannot have any justification in itself. Its value derives from the end for which it is employed."[16]

---

11 Juan Luis Segundo, *The Liberation of Theology* (Maryknoll, NY: Orbis Books, 1975), 106.

12 Segundo, *Liberation of Theology*, 116.

13 Segundo, *Liberation of Theology*, 110.

14 Segundo, *Liberation of Theology*, 154–82.

15 Segundo, *Liberation of Theology*, 166.

16 Segundo, *Liberation of Theology*, 171.

Thus Jesus's demonstration of service and love, and the general biblical directive against killing, are "equivalent to saying that one could not kill without a justifiable reason."[17]

Would commitment to liberation pacifism affect how we behave in the public arena? Would our peace witness be at risk?

I have resisted Burkholder's implication that liberation pacifists Neufeld and Snyder (much less Laverne Rutschman and Perry Yoder) are reluctant to uphold nonviolence as a norm in revolutionary contexts: Neufeld because of insufficient evidence and lack of definition of a key term, and Snyder because of his categorical statement that the right kind of nonviolence is relevant for the whole world. (Perry Yoder not only makes the same distinction Snyder has made between obedient [militant] nonviolence and disobedient [passive] nonviolence, he also distinguishes between use of force, which is legitimate, and lethal violence, which is not. He strongly affirms that "as Christians we are to be committed to working toward shalom militantly, but nonviolently."[18] He doubts whether one can credibly argue "on the one hand that shalom means the removal of violence and oppression and on the other that it is compatible with violence, can be brought about by violence."[19])

I have further suggested that perhaps Míguez Bonino and Pixley better fit this type, and that Segundo has already crossed the line into a more traditional justified violence position. Assuming that some Mennonites share the views of Míguez Bonino and Pixley, would this affect our mission strategy and put our peace witness at risk? Perhaps the best way to answer would be to identify how this type departs from traditional Mennonite thinking about nonviolence. I will identify five points:

1. This type puts greater emphasis on the efficacy and relevance of mission efforts. If justice, peace, salvation (liberation, emancipation), and reconciliation are the goals that fuel the fire of Christian service, how does one measure success except by reference to these? If no improvement is evident, or if things are getting worse, does this not justify a shift in strategy (ethics)? Traditionally Mennonites have emphasized obedience over success:

---

17 Segundo, *Liberation of Theology*, 166.

18 Perry B. Yoder, *Shalom: The Bible's Word for Salvation, Justice, and Peace* (Newton, KS: Faith and Life Press, 1987), 145.

19 P. Yoder, *Shalom*, 144.

our social responsibility is to be obedient to God, to maintain purity. But this type calls for increased involvement in achieving our stated goals of justice, peace, salvation, reconciliation.

2. This type sees the sovereignty of God manifest in history primarily through social structures, and secondarily in the obedient church. It is more confidently theocratic; it assumes that God uses social and political structures to achieve divine purposes in the world. Mennonites have not traditionally believed that society will be transformed from above, by rulers, and have held instead that God's primary tool for social transformation is the obedient church.

3. This type is more confident that Jesus is Lord of the world as well as the church. It affirms that "secular" obedience is also godly and advances the building of the kingdom. Mennonites have tended to see the realm of reality beyond the obedient church as the realm of evil, under Satan's sovereignty, "outside the perfection of Christ." The conviction that Christ is Lord of all leads to greater optimism about making a difference in the world; the traditional Mennonite view is more pessimistic about the possibility of radical change in secular society.

4. This type, though it pretends to reject all dichotomies, in fact creates its own. It suspects that the obedience of faith will not influence secular reality, and creates a dichotomy that calls for distinct strategies in the different realms of faith and unfaith. Mennonites have believed the obedience of faith will ultimately affect secular reality. Hence their insistence that the public ethic and the private ethic must be congruent.

5. This type claims to be more realistic about the degree to which all people (including obedient Christians) are implicated in violent structures. Total nonviolence does not exist because our lives are involved in violence at every turn; our ethic is compromised. Mennonites have tended not to recognize our complicity in perpetuating evil structures. Isolation, emigration, and silence have been important weapons in defense of ethical purity.

Personal reflections

At this point my "objective" analysis gives way to personal reflections. I hope license will be granted.

I am writing this document in Bogotá, Colombia, in the autumn of 1989. In the short time that this response has been in progress, more than 70 bombs have exploded in this city, many within hearing and window-rattling range of our apartment. Often my reflections have been interrupted by machine-gun fire. Our Canadian embassy has suggested that we not be too conspicuous—difficult instructions when one of our sons is a lively, blue-eyed, blond boy, and another is six-feet-two-inches tall and towers over Colombian crowds. We have armed or military escorts for virtually every detail of normal living—getting on and off airplanes, banking, buying groceries, obtaining government documents, going for walks or to church meetings after dark. The only way to avoid military protection would be to leave the country.

It has become increasingly clear to me that what is overt in Colombia is just as powerfully (although more covertly) present in the United States and Canada. There, too, we live under the daily protection of military weapons and police. It takes only a terrorist crisis in Quebec to invoke the War Measures Act, or a Kent State demonstration to rally the troops against US citizens. Tranquility and peace are only a façade. Hidden behind the surface lies the reality that nationhood is ultimately based on violence. What does nonviolence mean in such settings?

Not participating in or benefiting from or being oppressed by secular violence appear to be options only to the blissfully ignorant. In opposing militarism, we do not wish it away. Míguez Bonino attempts to help us by restating the issue: "The question is not whether we accept violence or not, but what do Christians do with the reality of violence in which we are all actively involved."[20] I would go beyond Míguez Bonino and say: The question is not, *Do we participate in violence?*, but, *What does nonviolence mean once we have acknowledged our participation in violence and our debt to the violence in our lives?* To put it more bluntly: *What does nonviolence mean in Bogotá when I am under daily military escort?* Some tentative suggestions:

1. All deliberation about nonviolence must begin with an acknowledgement and a confession of our participation in violence. To embrace nonviolence is not to annul our complicity in violent

---

20 Míguez Bonino, "On Discipleship, Justice and Power," 138.

structures. Paradoxically, the choice is not between nonviolence and militarism, or between nonviolence and violence. In ethical terms, human reality is such that the opposite of nonviolence is not violence but loyalty to violence as the best response to social problems. In biblical terms, this loyalty to and confidence in violent solutions is called idolatry. Our ethical struggle, then, is how to be nonviolent within militarism and within violence.

2. The credibility of the Anabaptist affirmation that all violence is evil is enhanced with each passing decade and century. It would be unfortunate if our tradition, which has seen this evil clearly and spoken against it loudly, would now retract this affirmation (either in doctrine or in practice). The search for nonviolent options is more and more relevant.

3. We should not see the liberation pacifist position as a threat. All of the liberation pacifist affirmations listed in the previous section (with the exception of the fourth) should be incorporated into Mennonite pacifism: relevance and efficacy are important in Christian witness, God is sovereign in social structures, Jesus is Lord of all creation, and we are complicit in violent structures. These emphases do not detract from but add to our traditional position.

4. The key to our discernment process is whether we speak from an abstract and theoretical perspective, or from a perspective of commitment and involvement. If the latter, we can be confident that we will find new, more creative, more effective and more faithful ways to promote peace and justice in the world. If the former, our deliberations amount to no more than a modern quest to discover how many angels can dance on the head of a pin.

Type 10

An Emerging Neo-sectarian Pacifism

Daniel Schipani

The provisional typology devised by John R. Burkholder identifies ten types of peace theology that have evolved among North American Mennonite and Brethren in Christ believers during the past 50 years ("Can We Make Sense of Mennonite Peace Theology?"). The typology functions as a heuristic instrument, helping us classify and assess diverse strains of peace theology on the Mennonite/Brethren in Christ scene.

Burkholder's reference to three generations of contributions suggests that we dare not overlook generational issues, broadly speaking, including psycho-sociological, cultural, political, religio-theological and other dynamics and agendas in concrete historical situations. By taking generational issues into consideration, we may be able to minimize the risk of talking past each other in our conversations on faith. (Indeed, the generational factor is perhaps at least one way to account for serious disagreements and misunderstandings in the Conversations/Dialogues on Faith held among Mennonites a few years ago.)

The case of Ted Koontz's reflections illustrates the merits of attending to Burkholder's suggestion about generational issues. Koontz's recent work, here discussed under Burkholder's original rubric, "Post-Political Pacifism," in most respects stands within the Guy F. Hershberger (first generation—"Historic Nonresistance") and John H. Yoder (second generation—"Messianic Community") traditions of Mennonite peace theology. Yet his work and thought reflect a different setting and vantage point, which Koontz explicitly deals with and assesses. In his piece on "Mennonites and the State: Preliminary Reflections," Koontz tells his personal story, and proposes some ways to address the issues brought into focus by the account of his pilgrimage.[1] His self-analysis and assessment are in themselves a creative contribution to the discussion, raising new questions and posing alternatives.

---

1 See Ted Koontz, "Mennonites and the State: Preliminary Reflections," in *Essays on Peace Theology and Witness*, edited by Willard H. Swartley (Elkhart, IN: Institute of Mennonite Studies, 1988), 35–60.

My references to this type of peace theology are qualified in two ways. First, Koontz presents his views on Mennonites and the state as preliminary reflections. Compared with other types under consideration in current discussions of Mennonite peace theologies, his contribution is in process, being developed, rather than standing as a definite and comprehensive formulation. So I refer to it in the title as an emerging strain.

Second, I regard the "Post-Political Pacifism" label originally given this type as inadequate. Burkholder's 1985 response to Koontz used the more apt label "Neo-Sectarian Realism." In light of Koontz's own pilgrimage and the analysis of his faith/intellectual journey, another appropriate label would be "post-ideological pacifism." This label draws on James Fowler's use of his faith development theory to look at theological types. Koontz's own narrative uses a developmental approach, beginning with naiveté and moving toward maturity. In Fowler's terms, an "ideological [peace] theology" would make the transition to Fowler's fourth stage by putting a premium on establishing and maintaining clear boundaries. This theology's language is intentionally passionate, appealing for new commitment and action based on such commitment. "A principal goal of theologies focused at Stage 4 is to bring about change. Whether intentional or not, the theologies focused at Stage 4 tend to have the characteristics of ideologies."[2]

Fowler then compares "ideological theologians" with "theologians of balance" (those making the transition to stage 5, moving beyond polarities and embracing paradox, attempting further integration) in terms of their differing views of the task of theology, of God's relation to history, of time and eschatology, of sin and evil. The "post-ideological" label points to the fact that Koontz has made a deliberate attempt to move beyond a crypto-Constantinian (liberal pacifist) ideological position, in order to reintegrate the two-kingdom ethic as well as a certain realism.

Analysis: Another two-kingdom ethic proposal

In a letter to Perry Yoder at Associated Mennonite Biblical Seminaries dated 15 April 1989 (discussing implications of the shift from "People of God" to "Kingdom [or Reign] of God" as a guiding principle for theological education), Koontz reiterated several key convictions that give us a clue

---

2 James W. Fowler, "Black Theologies of Liberation: A Structural-Developmental Analysis," in *The Challenge of Liberation Theology: A First World Response*, edited by Brian Mahan and L. Dale Richesin (Maryknoll, NY: Orbis Books, 1981), 83.

to his overall thinking concerning church and society, and hence a perspective from which to consider his paper on Mennonites and the state:

> I am increasingly convinced that we must always think not only in "dualist" terms (i.e. either church/world or old age/new age—other labels could be used) but in terms that take account of three fundamental realities—the "world" (the present order which is "fallen" and does not profess to accept the Lordship of Christ), the church (that body which in the present does acknowledge the Lordship of Christ and which, despite its fallenness, through grace imperfectly seeks to live in accordance with that Lordship), and the Kingdom (the inbreaking of God's reign through the church and through various redemptive events/movements/people outside the church, and which will come fully in the future as God brings it about).... We are not only to hope for/work for/expect a new world, but to begin living it now (certainly in partial and imperfect ways) among the community of faith.

Koontz's main understandings regarding the church and the state and society appear in the context of the reformulation of a two-kingdom ethic. Such a reformulation includes the key claims and principles (in the sense of implications or guidelines for faithful practice and reflection) of his emerging perspective. Those claims and principles are as follows:

On the nature and role of the church

1. The church is God's primary vehicle for acting in history. The ecclesial community has been called to live as an alternative social reality. Its primary means of achieving social change is by creating new and more liberated models of life. Therefore, political involvement outside the ecclesial realm must be seen as derivative from and subordinated to the wider mission work of witness and service, though political involvement is potentially legitimate and even desirable.

2. The church's faithfulness in its own life and mission is essential to its more direct "political" witness. This is a matter of integrity, truthfulness and credibility. The church's call to embody the kingdom-like alternatives of freedom, justice and peace must be

given priority attention by those concerned with witness to the government. In other words, the primary political agenda must be the historical and concrete reality (i.e., ecclesial structure, relationships, values and practices, etc.) of the faith community that professes and claims to live according to the rule of Christ. At stake is the question of faithfulness as well as consistency and even relevance.

3. Agape is the overarching behavioral norm for the church, in current as well as ultimate terms. That is, Koontz maintains and restates the traditional Anabaptist-Mennonite affirmation regarding Jesus' ethic of sacrificial love. This affirmation leaves no room for distinction—or dualism—between current and ultimate agape claims as far as the church is concerned.

On the nature and role of the state

1. The state must be taken seriously on its own terms. In God's economy, the state is an ever-present reminder of human fallenness and rebellion. Its function is different from that of the church, hence (in a notable departure from Yoder's "Messianic Community" approach) the emphasis on respecting the integrity of the state's character "on its own terms."

2. Government is the institution that has primary responsibility for dealing with the consequences of human fallenness. A central function of government is to protect the innocent and restrain evildoers. That is, the state has been charged with confronting concrete expressions of sin, e.g., exploitation and other forms of oppression and violence by various actors. Koontz calls this "primary sin which necessarily pulls down the performance of the state."[3] From this it follows that:

3. "An appropriate ethic for the state is different from an appropriate ethic for the church."[4] Even as one affirms that God ultimately has one will for all peoples and institutions that is, life according to Jesus' ethic—a clear qualification must be made concerning the situation and function of the state in the real world. In our fallen world a moral standard other than agape

---

3 T. Koontz, "Mennonites and the State," 49.

4 T. Koontz, "Mennonites and the State," 48.

is needed to guide state behavior. Because of historical conditions of systemic evil and radical sin, the state's behavior can be labeled "sinful" on one level (e.g., as violent and coercive, thus falling short of the ultimate norm revealed in Jesus), and "right," or at least adequate, on another level (e.g., when it restrains further evil, protects the good, or enhances community). Therefore, some kind of "ethic of fallenness" needs to be developed. Further, we require "middle axioms" or norms other than agape, in order to promote the state or society's movement toward agape.

4. "The proper norm for the state is to protect the good by restraining evildoers with the least possible coercion or violence."[5] This is a relative norm which calls for careful discernment of different kinds of state action, including violence. The norm further assumes that the state may be too pacifistic in certain situations (e.g., by failing to deter or restrain evildoers), and that governments are morally required to promote and nurture the political community so that the amount of force needed to protect the good can be decreased. Using a model similar to those developed by John H. Yoder in *The Christian Witness to the State*,[6] Koontz in a helpful way summarizes his position on norms for the state:[7]

---

5 T. Koontz, "Mennonites and the State," 50.

6 John Howard Yoder, *The Christian Witness to the State* (Newton, KS: Faith and Life Press, 1964), 60-73.

7 T. Koontz, "Mennonites and the State," 53.

118 | Mennonite Peace Theology

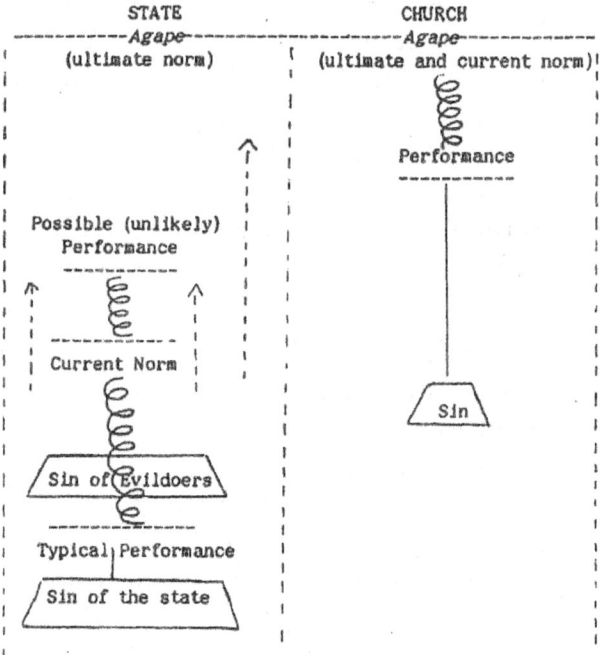

Figure 10.1

Koontz explains the model, as follows:

> The arrow on the upper right represents the pull toward the ultimate norm of agape (or at least nonviolence) inherent in the model as the state must take seriously the "least possible" part of the norm in working to create a community in which cohesion is maintained on the basis of consent and common bonds rather than coercion and violence. The "Possible (unlikely) Performance" line illustrates a situation (normally but not always hypothetical) where the state uses too little coercion or violence and because of this fails to protect the good. The "Current Norm" line is the actual, relative norm which the state should use at the moment—restraint of evil with the least possible coercion or violence. Note that this norm is itself moveable [sic], as stressed in the text and as illustrated by the arrows on both sides of the Current Norm.

Where this Current Norm actually is in any specific case will depend on how heavy the weight of Sin of Evildoers is, because this determines how much violence is needed to restrain. evil. Thus, how far this current, relative norm is from the absolute norm of agape depends on the minimum possible coercion or violence needed to protect the good in a given situation. The "Sin of Evildoers" weight is what holds the "Current Norm" down. That is, the actual norm which the state should act on at the moment in a given case is pulled down from the absolute norm of agape to the extent that evildoers threaten the good in ways which can only be restrained by state coercion or violence. The distance between the Current Norm and the Typical Performance of the state (represented here by the "spring" between them) is due to the state's own sin and is a measure of its sinfulness. As illustrated here, normally (almost always) the sin of the state pulls it farther from agape, by using more violence than necessary or by supporting evildoers instead of the good. But as suggested earlier, it also is possible to fail to be a good state by being too close to agape in actual performance in a particular case (thereby failing to protect the good), though never in an effort to move the Current Norm (and the corresponding immediate "right" action) closer to agape so that protection of the good can be accomplished using less violent or coercive means.

I am drawn to this kind of model for thinking about norms for the state because (1) it seems to me congruent with biblical material which does not, I think, either implicitly or explicitly call the state to the same standard to which it calls Christian disciples, (2) it does justice to my own sense of the dilemmas which statesmen sometimes face and does not ask them, as statesmen, to follow the norm of agape in a fallen situation (though we should also call statesmen as individuals to become Christians and, if there is no consistent way to be both Christian and statesman in a particular situation, to stop being statesmen), and (3) it allows plenty of room for a prophetic critique of government. These first two reasons seem to me to be in basic continuity with "traditional" Mennonite thought. But the third, I think, is radically different from the church/world dualism in Mennonite ethics which many recent writers have criticized, a dualism which saw the world as fallen and therefore sometimes appeared to feel there was nothing to say to the state by way of prophetic critique. I agree with those who wish to speak a prophetic word to government. What I have sought to do is to begin exploring the normative framework out of which such a prophetic critique should come, a framework which recognizes that the state's function in God's economy is different from that of the church.[8]

Questions about this emerging type

The stance of realism Koontz advocates becomes problematic at several points, beginning with his understanding of the "facts," which is then manifested in his specific moral and political judgments. As Ted Grimsrud has pointed out, one wonders whether the perspectives or "facts" Koontz deals with are the facts of the powerful rather than the facts of the majority of the people in the world or even in North America.[9] Koontz does not seem to take into account the perspectives of the oppressed and disenfranchised, the victims of the state's economic or justice systems, for example. One also wonders whether this two-kingdom ethic belongs to the tradition that accepts the "real world" of socio-political power as inevitably limited to power politics.

A related concern is that the emphasis on realistic political assessment at global, national or other levels, though rightly suspicious of optimistic views of political activity, seems to preclude radical prophetic, "utopian" witness to the state and society, witness inspired and sustained by the vision of the coming reign of God, of shalom. The passion for justice (which Koontz does not define) has been left behind. The paper does not explicitly address the basis or orientation of such a witness, or identify the source of middle axioms or other more specific criteria.

---

8 T. Koontz, "Mennonites and the State," 53-54.

9 Ted Grimsrud, "Response to Ted Koontz's Paper: Mennonites and the State," Peace Theology Colloquium IV, 20-23 June 1985, Elkhart, Indiana.

Koontz's understanding of the central function of the state in a fallen world, and what the church can expect from the state, merits more discussion. We need to examine Koontz's "ethic of fallenness" for the state (e.g., the matter of sinful yet right state violent/coercive action), looking specifically at its biblical hermeneutical base. To date, Koontz's reflection on this point is provocative, and in significant discontinuity with John Yoder's.

Peace Theology Colloquium IV in June 1985 identified eschatology as a crucial theological issue for understanding church-state relations: there are differing judgments about the extent to which the kingdom is already or is likely to be a present reality, the kind of eschatology that takes the resurrection seriously, and how we frame positively a two-kingdom viewpoint in which Christians speak to and participate in the state.[10] More specifically, how do we move from emphasis on restraining evil to actual peacemaking and justice-doing? Koontz's emerging neo-sectarian or neo-ideological pacifism needs to be challenged also along these lines.

Koontz's reformulation of a two-kingdom ethic reintroduces the Constantinian-sectarian church polarity. How can we move beyond that polarity to envision a way of being the church in the world in the present historical situation?

Koontz claims that the church is God's primary vehicle for acting in history. The practical question recurs: How can we make the content of that claim more of a reality? How can actual communities move more concretely and faithfully toward becoming viable social and political alternatives in our world? One hopes that further work and reflection in the light of this type of Mennonite peace theology will address this challenge.

---

10 See Gayle Gerber Koontz and Perry Yoder, "Issues and Questions Raised during the IMS-MCC Peace Colloquium," in *Essays on Peace Theology and Witness*, edited by Willard H. Swartley (Elkhart, IN: Institute of Mennonite Studies, 1985), 210.

Further Reflections

Reflections on Mennonite Uses of Anabaptist History

Arnold Snyder

John R. Burkholder has summarized the history of twentieth-century Mennonite thought on peace using four categories: (1) nonresistance as foundation, (2) expanding the theological dimensions, (3) new church-state thinking, and (4) the conservative reaction.[1] As a historian of the sixteenth century, I regret to see that, according to Burkholder, the Anabaptist theological heritage was actively operative as a dialogical partner in only the first of these four—and at best latently operative in the remaining three. I believe Burkholder's description is correct.

It is well known that "the recovery of the Anabaptist vision" played a crucial role in Mennonite self-definition in the early decades of the twentieth century. Some version of normative Anabaptism is still appealed to by virtually all Mennonites, across the entire spectrum of positions on peace issues. Unfortunately, however, among historians there is no longer a commonly accepted view of what normative Anabaptism might be. Current historical wisdom has it that "normative Anabaptism" was the product of denominational (Mennonite) apologetic historiography. Contemporary historians' description of Anabaptism is of a multifaceted movement, pacifist in some manifestations, reluctantly pacifist in others (hand on the sword-hilt until the Lord comes) and nonpacifist in still others. Current Mennonite theology has yet to come to terms with this polymorphic and polygenetic understanding of Anabaptism.

In spite of J. Denny Weaver's recent efforts in *Becoming Anabaptist*, it is not at all clear how—or even whether—recent Anabaptist historiography can serve the Mennonite Church.[2] The polymorphic reality of sixteenth-century Anabaptism is not edifying in a normative or prescriptive way. Hence Weaver's problems in the final chapter of his book, where he

---

1 J. R. Burkholder, "Can We Make Sense out of Mennonite Peace Theology?" Working draft presented at the joint meeting of the MCC Peace Committee and Ecumenical Peace Theology Working Group, 3-4 November 1989, Elkhart, Indiana; reprinted in the present volume.

2 J. Denny Weaver, *Becoming Anabaptist: The Origin and Significance of Sixteenth-Century Anabaptism* (Scottdale, PA: Herald Press, 1987).

tries (without success, in my view) to derive normative guidelines from a relativizing historiography.

It seems to me that theological projects purporting to be rooted in Anabaptism ought to begin by recovering the Anabaptist visions of the sixteenth century in all their confusing multiplicity. This is an important first step because the word *Anabaptism* continues to connote a vague Swiss normativity, contrary to the historical facts. A quick review reveals at least the following varieties:

1. Realpolitik (Balthasar Hubmaier)
2. Apocalyptic, provisional pacifism (Hans Hut)
3. Holy war (Bernhard Rothmann—Münster)
4. Absolute dualistic pacifism (Swiss Anabaptists and Hutterites)
5. Moderate dualistic pacifism (Pilgram Marpeck, Menno Simons)
6. Spiritualist pacifism (Hans Denk, Leonhard Schiemer, Hans Schlaffer)

I find it intellectually unsatisfying, and unnecessarily limiting, to do peace theology exclusively on the basis of numbers 4 and 5 above, as if the rest were not genuinely Anabaptist. From a historical point of view, the conclusion does not hold up. Hubmaier was without question the most significant and seminal Anabaptist thinker on questions of baptism, for instance. Rothmann was Anabaptist enough that Marpeck reissued a slightly cleaned up version of one of his major writings. Hut was the most successful Anabaptist evangelist in the first generation. And so on. We need to look again at what the theological core of Anabaptism might be by allowing all positions to speak and inform, rather than by bracketing out positions we do not find immediately edifying. When all is said and done, we may well want to affirm what Bender affirmed as the truest, most biblical course for the Mennonite church, but it is not historically credible anymore simply to affirm a supposed Anabaptist peace position to which we wish to be faithful.

A second and related point: it seems to me that one byproduct of the modern Mennonite focus on the Schleitheim confession (article VI, on the sword) has been that we subsume pastoral and spiritual questions under the heading of ethics. This in turn has profound consequences for our peace theology. A survey of Mennonite writing on peace in the twentieth century reveals the operative words to have been *discipleship*, *obedience, community*. Only rarely is *yieldedness*, for example, referred to in connection with our theology of peace. Schleitheim, representing the Swiss tradition, is strongly biblicist and ethical: we make peace because Jesus did and because he told us to follow him. Schleitheim, however, says nothing about how we are to achieve this peaceful state when confronted with injustice, torture, and potential martyrdom. The historical record testifies amply that the Anabaptists did find the spiritual resources to be true to the call of discipleship. How were they enabled to live as faithful disciples? The ethical prescription, which merely enjoins obedience, was certainly not in itself an adequate source of enablement.

Our peace theology to date has aided us in thinking through the biblical bases for peacemaking, clarifying church-state questions, and creating a space for nonviolent resistance (as opposed to our more traditional, passive nonresistance). We owe a debt of gratitude to those who have struggled to open the Mennonite church to the possibility of working for social justice. But for whatever reasons, our theology about peace has had little to say at the level of elucidating a spirituality of peacemaking. Curiously enough, I find many more resources for this task in the writings of Guy F. Hershberger and others of his time and in the *Sword and Trumpet / Guidelines for Today* group. Perhaps we progressives have been embarrassed by the overt piety required to deal with questions of this kind. At any rate, I believe we can no longer shunt such questions aside. How are we equipping ourselves spiritually and pastorally for the task of peacemaking in our communities and abroad? Do we have a realistic awareness of the profound inner resources we will need if we are to be able to yield our lives in love for our brothers and sisters?

I may be guilty of extrapolating too much from my own experience. I confess that discipleship, as I understood it, took me to Nicaragua. But it did not enable me to love Contras. If I understand Jesus, he asks the latter of me; out of such love discipleship will grow as fruit from a healthy tree. I believe the most pressing theological need in our church is the cultivation of a spirituality and worship life that supports nonviolent discipleship.

We possess valuable resources in our Anabaptist tradition that can help us refocus the spiritual and liturgical dimensions of peace theology. If we widen our vision of Anabaptism to include the South Germans and others, we will discover that a deep spirituality sustained not only their peacemaking but the entire Anabaptist enterprise, from baptism on. These mystical Anabaptists believed the crucial struggle was to yield completely and continually to Christ. Only then would they be able to act in love—motivated by the living Spirit, having the mind of Christ—even in situations of violence.

We will profit from meditating deeply on what the Anabaptists said about yielding to the renewing Spirit of God. The profound historical fact that Anabaptists faced martyrdom nonviolently, that they accepted horrible suffering, that they endured economic oppression: these are subjects that warrant more attention in our historical and theological deliberations. Such study would be fruitful particularly as we sail farther out on the seas of acculturation. I hope, for instance, that by the time the second edition of Duane Friesen's fine book appears, the important concluding chapter on spiritual resources for peacemaking will include some Anabaptist examples alongside those of Gandhi and King.[3]

I am not proposing another incarnation of H. S. Bender's magnificent project of recovery; the time for that is long past. But I am painfully aware, as I work in my little corner of the Swiss historical vineyard, that our church is being ill-served by the illusion that we know our Anabaptist history pretty well, thank you. In fact, I would say we had barely begun to dialogue with our history when we concluded that there was no more there for us. On the contrary, I believe that a visionary theological project will require sustained dialogue with the past, not a mere cursory nod in the general direction of our Anabaptist forebears.

---

3 Duane K. Friesen, *Christian Peacemaking and International Conflict: A Realist Pacifist Perspective* (Scottdale, PA: Herald Press, 1986), 225-53.

Shalom Political Theology

A New Type of Mennonite Peace Theology for a New Era of Discipleship

Malinda Elizabeth Berry

Introduction

In my office I have a small stack of photocopied booklets with black plastic comb binding and cream-colored card stock for the cover.* On several occasions I have used this modest publication—*Mennonite Peace Theology: A Panorama of Types*[1]—as a textbook, making sure to have a least one extra copy on hand because it is not easy to come by. What I have found so useful about this simple collection of essays is that it makes undergraduate students open their eyes wide in wonder. It raises a question they never thought to ask: Is there more than one way to be a Mennonite pacifist?

This booklet opened my eyes and heart, and this expository essay is both a homage to the *Panorama* and an offering of a new form of Mennonite peace theology—shalom political theology (hereafter SPT)—that has grown from my grounding in the traditions of Mennonite peace theologies, plural.[2] What follows affirms the importance of cultivating a variety of peace theology types, and builds on the original typology by offering SPT as a synergistic blend of some of the lesser-known types featured in the *Panorama* with the hope that Historic Peace Churches (hereafter

---

* Malinda Elizabeth Berry is associate professor of theology and ethics at Anabaptist Mennonite Biblical Seminary in Elkhart, Indiana. This essay was first published in *The Conrad Grebel Review* 34, no. 1 (Winter 2016): 49–73, and is reprinted here with permission.
1 John Richard Burkholder and Barbara Nelson Gingerich, eds., *Mennonite Peace Theology: A Panorama of Types* (Akron, PA: Mennonite Central Committee Peace Office, 1991).
2 I have developed the initial form of shalom political theology (SPT) in Malinda Elizabeth Berry, "'This Mark of a Standing Human Figure Poised to Embrace': A Constructive Theology of Social Responsibility, Nonviolence and Nonconformity" (Ph.D. diss., Union Theological Seminary, New York, 2013). This essay both revises and adds to my original discussion, and significant portions of it are drawn directly from that longer work.

HPCs) will continue to use their unique forms of theologizing to align with God's reconciling purposes and vision in the world.[3]

The Case for a New Type and its Components

Why is there a need for a new form of peace theology? Aren't ten types sufficient? Well, no. In broad terms, lived theology, which Mennonite peace theology is, is constantly in dialogue with the world around it, requiring articulations of how a biblical vision of peace is central to Christian faith. My offering alone does not meet this requirement, because while our working typology has included voices influenced by experiences from around the world, as John A. Lapp notes in his preface to the *Panorama*, our typology has yet to include and be reliant on African, Asian, Australian, and Latin American voices.[4] More specifically, there are three reasons for expanding the ten types.

First, for understandable reasons Mennonite peace theology has been a discourse dominated by men's voices, perspectives, and personal narratives. The *Panorama* is a case in point. While women participated in the consultation that led to the booklet's publication, only two of the ten contributors were women, and even then, women were not identified as proponents of any of the types of peace theology under scrutiny.[5] This gender imbalance is a moral problem in light of the denominational Confession of Faith in a Mennonite Perspective. Article 6 articulates a theological anthropology that understands women and men as "equally and wonderfully made in the divine image," with Article 15 affirming that the Holy Spirit calls both women and men to be leaders in the church.[6] Because we have these convictions about women, it is important that women's voices, perspectives, and personal narratives actively shape our tradition.

---

3 By "Historic Peace Churches" I refer to the Church of the Brethren, Mennonites, and the Society of Friends, a cluster of denominations that understand themselves to be pacifistic.

4 John A. Lapp, preface to Mennonite Peace Theology: A Panorama of Types.

5 Three notable works that are part correctives to this trend include Elizabeth Yoder, ed., *Peace Theology and Violence against Women* (Elkhart, IN: Institute of Mennonite Studies, 1992); Rosalee Bender et al., *Piecework: A Women's Peace Theology* (Winnipeg: Mennonite Central Committee Canada, 1997); and Carol Penner, "Mennonite Silences and Feminist Voices: Peace Theology and Violence against Women" (Ph.D. diss., University of St. Michael's College, Toronto, 1999).

6 "Article 6. Creation and Calling of Human Beings" and "Article 15. Ministry and Leadership," Confession of Faith in a Mennonite Perspective, http://mennoniteusa.org/confession-of-faith/ ministry-and-leadership/.

I am putting forward SPT as a feminist approach to Mennonite peace theology.[7]

Second, historical dimensions have had contextual sway in shaping Mennonite peace theology types. For example, the post-World War II project of making pacifism intellectually respectable was one that consumed HPC scholars. As a junior scholar, I observe that today we do not have a well-defined or obvious scholarly community that sees itself as charged with the task of keeping peace theology alive for subsequent generations in the same way as those featured in the *Panorama*. That is, having established Anabaptist-informed pacifism as an intellectually respectable Christian stance, it is appropriate to consider how moments like the end of the Cold War, the advent of the War on Terrorism, the global recognition of the Green Belt Movement, #BlackLivesMatter, and the long-overdue closures of Indian residential/boarding schools and Magdalene laundries become points of interest for HPCs in light of decades of political advocacy for alternatives to military service in wartime. Thus I put forward SPT as a member of Generation X, interested in how both church and society are faring as our social and institutional lives change dramatically and rapidly.

Third, the pacifism of the Messianic community (Type 5 in the *Panorama*) is arguably the most common form of peace theology among US Mennonites. One of its weaknesses is that it is insufficient for helping contemporary Anabaptist communities make theological sense of social problems that indict the church for its inability to stand with the oppressed.[8] While several other types in the *Panorama* work to address this weakness (i.e., social responsibility, radical pacifism, realist pacifism, and liberation pacifism), the prominence of scholarship in the tradition of John Howard Yoder translates into limited debate about methodological blind spots in the pacifism of the Messianic community. This provides another reason for my arguing for SPT: to disrupt the hegemonic qualities of our peace theological discourse.

---

7 Throughout this essay, I use "feminist" as an umbrella term for critical woman-centered approaches to theological and ethical concerns that includes both global feminist perspectives and US movements of Asian American feminism, black feminism, womanism, Latina feminism, mujerista, native feminism, and white feminism.

8 A few high-profile examples include clergy sexual abuse cases in the Roman Catholic Church, the HIV/AIDS crisis in the Black Church, Christians on either side of the marriage equality/ sanctity of marriage debate, and climate change denials centered in Evangelical groups.

This essay has three parts. Part one weaves together James Evans's work on social problems as theological problems and Dorothee Soelle's work with mystical political theology. This section gives the reader a way to anchor my use of political theology in the sea of books, essays, and articles that are also concerned with where, how, why, and to what effect our God-talk meets various forms of political concern. Part two develops the biblical warrant for SPT. My argument is that through the perspective of wisdom literature, biblical shalom is linked to the theological motifs of Creation, the prophetic oracles of the Peaceable Kingdom, and Jesus' proclamation of the *basileia tou Theou* (the kingdom of God). This continuity becomes the synergistic hermeneutic that focuses peace theology as form of theological wisdom.

Part three is a constructive proposal for SPT, along with examples of how SPT can interrogate and re-shape the theo-ethical life of faith communities in ways that peace theology has not historically done. I direct my proposal to communities of Christians persuaded that peace, justice, and nonviolence are central to faith, values, and ethics; those communities may be ecumenical or denominationally particular. SPT integrates the principles of theological anthropology, nonviolence, and nonconformity as I have come to articulate them through my encounters with Reinhold Niebuhr, Martin Luther King, Jr., and Doris Janzen Longacre.[9]

I should make a methodological comment here. SPT is not "biblical theology" in the classic, disciplinary sense of the term. Nor is SPT primarily a systematics or a particular theological ethic. SPT is a constructive theological offering that integrates three dimensions of confessional discourse—biblical study, theological reflection, and ethical engagement—into a biblical theoethic of shalom manifesting as discipleship committed to nonviolence and nonconformity.

Political Theology and Peace Theology

Because God loves the world, to love and serve God is to embrace and serve the world God loves. Such a confession is political, calling us to

---

9 Martin Luther King, Jr. was unfaithful to his spouse Coretta Scott King. Scholars have documented this aspect of King's life, and I am grateful for their fact-finding and analysis. As a feminist Christian, I am uneasy about drawing on and using King as a source for my work, knowing that he used patriarchal privilege to dominate women. I hold this tension by naming his failings, reading him critically, and striving to direct readers' attention to him not as an exemplar but as one who contributed ideas to the public sphere of Christian theology and ethics that are worth learning from and adapting in light of his transgressions.

account for how we believe God does or does not sanction our human polities and enactments of human power. Political theological confession involves looking outwardly and inwardly, and also involves dialogical communication and multivalent awareness that keeps outward and inward realities in conversation with each other. An inward glance that turns outward might raise the question, How is God present in my life, and what difference does God's love make in how I see the world? Peering outwardly to contemplate public policy dilemmas can shape internal conversations in faith communities and how they do or do not use power equitably. Such confession has led me to consider theologians James H. Evans, Jr. and Dorothee Soelle, both because their work expands what we typically think of as political theology and because it is shaped by their outward and inward seeing commensurate with social justice hermeneutics endemic to Mennonite peace theology. In many ways the term "political theology" is trendy, and therefore requires unpacking. However, I will limit my discussion to how Evans's and Soelle's uses of it shape how I employ political theology as the discursive framework for SPT.[10]

In short, Evans links social problems to practical theology and political theology through African American experience, both chastening political theology and calling for a hermeneutics of suspicion of ourselves, lest we think too highly of the state and too little of the church or vice versa. He helps SPT call Mennonite communities to account for the moments when power in the Messianic community goes unchecked, protecting members who act sinfully and thinking the state cannot be an agent of God's justice. Similarly, Soelle calls for a hermeneutics of suspicion in order to reclaim a form of Christian piety that recognizes how God-talk also functions as political speech. Her particular contribution to SPT comes from bringing her exploration of mysticism to bear on social problems and their relationship to the ego, possessions, and violence. She posits that we are all mystics, making "God desires fullness of life for all" the central theological basis for distinguishing between false and genuine mysticism.[11] I will now explicate these two writers' perspectives and contributions to SPT in more detail.

As Evans describes how his book *We Shall All Be Changed: Social Problems and Theological Renewal* is a work of practical theology, he says that

---

10 Readers interested in my detailed analysis and evaluation of political theology may want to consult my dissertation.

11 Dorothee Soelle, *The Silent Cry: Mysticism and Resistance*, trans. Barbara Rumscheidt (Minneapolis: Fortress Press, 2001), 52–55.

his interest is in offering a deeply theological response to persistent social problems, because how we expect Christian witness to interact with such problems is complicated and requires sustained theological analysis.[12] But he is not interested in simply analyzing social problems; he wants to address what he calls "two deeply felt needs": a public longing for spiritual renewal and a similar longing for common ground through social transformation.

As I survey the global landscape, I concur with Evans. From climate change and critiques of the industrial food system to hidden but persistent human trafficking and sexual violence, from gun violence at home and drone attacks far away to shrinking congregations and growing religiously motivated violence, it does not take long for social justice-oriented Christians to wonder exactly how God is making all things new in our time. Evans argues that these two desires, spiritual renewal and social transformation, are not only deeply felt but deeply connected.[13] As he makes his case for understanding what links social problems, spiritual renewal, and social transformation, he offers valuable commentary on how practical theology's discourse is related to other kinds of God-talk, notably political theology. Evans argues that by developing an awareness of social problems, however immediate or removed they are from our most direct experiences, we have new access to questions about ultimate reality. "Face to face with God, the theological dimensions of social problems are brought to light," he says, "and the social dimensions of theological problems become apparent."[14]

Evans laments the persistent majority of theologians who do not consider social problems and dilemmas to be their bailiwick. If and when those problems do enter theological conversations, he contends, they do so under the umbrella of ethics, to which he makes this objection: "Assigning discussion of social problems in theological discourse solely to the field of ethics does justice to neither the field of ethics nor the influence of these problems on Christian witness in our times."[15] At best, such a

---

12 James H. Evans Jr., *We Shall All Be Changed: Social Problems and Theological Renewal* (Minneapolis: Fortress Press, 1997), v.

13 Evans, *We Shall All Be Changed*, 89-90.

14 Evans, *We Shall All Be Changed*, 10. In making his case, Evans appropriates Gordon Kaufman's concept of mystery, which Evans describes as "the name we give to our ongoing attempts to find meaning in and solutions to those human problems that appear to be timeless, permanent, novel, contemporary, but always intractable" (11).

15 Evans, *We Shall All Be Changed*, 1.

disconnect makes ethical action merely habitual and reflexive: Christians simply respond to their enemies with love without a second thought because that is what Christians are supposed to do. At worst, without offering a deeper spirituality or moral grounding beyond a basic biblicism, Christians' actions may be ethical in an objective sense but not in a subjective sense, because their actions lack the basic theological reflection that goes hand-in-glove with ethics.

Theology in its broadest sense, Evans argues, is a combination of three different but closely related elements: fundamental or foundational theology, systematic theology, and practical theology.[16] From the German schools, Evans cites Friedrich Schleiermacher and Gerhard Ebeling. The former considered practical theology to be the aspects of theological education that give the organization and structure of the church's life as a polity and a community. The latter argued that practical theology is the theory giving form and shape to church leadership, compared to other disciplines of theological education providing the content of that leadership. Evans contrasts this German perspective with those of John Macquarrie (United Kingdom) and David Tracy (United States), both of whom grant practical theology a wider definition: it is concerned with "the ecclesiastical life of the community."[17]

Evans notes that both Macquarrie and Tracy define practical theology in a way that aligns it with political theology. Political theology is a theological discourse that explores Christian understanding of how God does or does not sanction human structuring of nation-states. Contemporary political theology also incorporates social analysis of human power dynamics as a vital part of its method. In this way, political theology is always going to reflect on institutions, and where political theologies part ways is in their view of the state. What Evans brings into the discussion is his concern about political theologies' tendency to collapse state and church. On one hand, Schleiermacher and Ebeling seem to take such a high view of the church that it becomes a "divinely ordered political community." On the other, Macquarrie and Tracy both assume that the state is a "justly ordered polis." It is at this point that Evans levels his critique, arguing that in the US "where African Americans have been oppressed by despotic notions of the state and excluded by truncated notions of the

---

16 Evans, *We Shall All Be Changed*, 2.

17 See John Macquarrie, *Principles of Christian Theology* (New York: Scribner, 1977), 127; and David Tracy, *The Analogical Imagination: Christian Theology and the Culture of Pluralism* (New York: Crossroad, 1981), 6ff.

church, theocracy or a narrow ecclesiasticism become suspect as points of departure for practical theology" and, I would add, for political theology.[18]

Dorothee Soelle's *The Silent Cry: Mysticism and Resistance* is another example of the paradigm Evans establishes. Her approach to political/practical theology is activist in its orientation but also mystical. And like Evans, she laments the split between theology and ethics. She shares his hope that our human imagination will grow stronger, so that we can unite our experiences of the world with how we live in the world.[19]

Soelle's intention in *The Silent Cry* is to integrate her mystical spiritual experiences, borne of everyday living, with her life in the academy and in the institutional church. In particular, she wants to correct the impression that mystics received their most profound insights in isolation. "Was the demeanor of flight from the world, separation, and solitude adequate for mysticism?" she asks. "Were there not also other forms of expressing mystical consciousness to be found in the life of communities as well as individuals?" Soelle concludes that we base many of our assumptions on a false distinction between the mystical as internal and the political as external. With a desire to repair this breech, she writes, "everything that is within needs to be externalized so it doesn't spoil, like the manna in the desert that was hoarded for future consumption." And there are models of mysticism that remind us that "there is no experience of God that can be so privatized that it becomes and remains the property of one owner, the privilege of a person of leisure, the esoteric domain of the initiated." From Soelle's perspective, our times call for mysticism imbued with a spirit of resistance and a passion for transformation—a declaration of No! in the face of injustice.[20]

By introducing mysticism into the discourse of political theology, Soelle hopes to contribute to personal healing and communal transformation.

> To read texts of mysticism is to have renewed cognition of one's self, of a being that is buried under rubble. Thus, the discovery of the mystical tradition also sets free one's own forgotten experience. . . . If it is true that God is love, then the separation of religion and ethics—or, in

---

18 Evans, *We Shall All Be Changed*, 2.

19 Soelle, *The Silent Cry: Mysticism and Resistance*, 5.

20 Soelle, *The Silent Cry: Mysticism and Resistance*, 3.

the technical terminology of the academy, the separation of systematic theology and social ethics—is dangerous as well as detrimental to both sides. It is self-destructive for religion and ethics because it empties religion, reducing its basis for experiencing the world. It turns ethics into arbitrary arrangements of individual tribes and hordes.[21]

In identifying the importance of the existential aspects of religious experience and the meaning of Christian faith, she is talking about the search for shalom.

Together, Evans and Soelle reinforce the deeply Anabaptist impulse to keep theology and ethics knitted together with a biblical view of the world. Through their unique paradigms of political theology, they also bring something new to conversations about peace theology: the multivalent dialogue between what we see when we look both outwardly beyond ourselves and inwardly at ourselves (as individuated people, tight-woven faith communities, minority subcultures). Evans's integration of spiritual renewal and social transformation, and Soelle's belief in mysticism's power to be a catalyst for personal healing and communal transformation, offer Mennonite peace theological discourse a theological framework for communal self-examination as a spiritual necessity.

As Anabaptist Christians, we regard our original sin as not equated with our nature but with the self-conscious choice for evil rather than good. Baptism, according to Pilgram Marpeck, marks our choice to crucify sin and experience resurrection and new life in Jesus Christ.[22] God's grace is present in our lives as a midwife, an agent of rebirth and regeneration. Psalm 34:14 comes to mind: "Depart from evil, and do good; seek peace, and pursue it." This is not a platitude but an invitation to seriously consider the theoethical challenges of shalom-oriented love and service united by the socially transformative and mystical pathway of God's politics: making peace as we seek justice by keeping our eyes focused outwardly and inwardly.

Theological Perspectives on Biblical Shalom

In Sunday school most of us learn that "shalom" is the Hebrew word for peace. What we tend not to learn is how holistic this peace is. "Peace"

---

21 Soelle, *The Silent Cry: Mysticism and Resistance*, 6.

22 Pilgram Marpeck, *The Writings of Pilgram Marpeck*, trans. William Klassen and Walter Klaassen (Scottdale, PA: Herald Press, 1978), 108ff.

is an important term, but the cultural baggage it carries in Mennonite communities has led me to give "Peace" a break. In opting instead for "shalom" I am signaling that SPT is interested in holistic theo-ethical education and formation. Peace theology is something academics offer to the church, so that together we might innovate a way of being missional that is both socially responsible and nonviolent.

Shalom is the principle that links prophetic testimony of the Peaceable Kingdom oracles, found in Isaiah and Hosea, with Jesus' prophetic proclamations about the basileia tou Theou, particularly in the Synoptic Gospels.[23] In this part of the essay I seek to establish a theological definition of shalom that serves as the foundation for SPT and supports the holistic formation of disciples who know how to respond nonviolently to conflict within and beyond the church, and to offer a credible Christian witness that empowers others to make the same commitment.

Four Dimensions of Shalom

In *Shalom: The Bible's Word for Salvation, Justice, and Peace*, Perry B. Yoder provides a four-part definition of the word that encapsulates God's intention for wholeness. In one sense, shalom refers to material wellbeing and economic prosperity. When we ask after someone's shalom—"How are you? How are your loved ones?"—we are asking after their health, financial situation, or even physical safety and security.[24] In a second sense, shalom refers to social relationships and God's desire for justice to permeate the interactions between neighbors and nations. Moreover, the presence of shalom gives rise to a feeling of God working to end suffering and oppression. "Thus," Yoder writes, "in the arena of human relations, we see that shalom describes the way things ought to be . . . [involving] a much wider and more positive state of affairs than a narrow understanding of peace as antiwar or antimilitary activity."[25]

In a third sense, shalom refers to moral and ethical dimensions of our lives. Persons of shalom act with integrity and speak straightforwardly, and their conduct is in stark contrast with oppressors who deceive and

---

23 Peaceable Kingdom references include passages like Isa. 2:2-4, 11:1-9, 65:17-25, and Hos. 2:15-20. A key theme is a cessation of violence between creatures who now have a predator/prey relationship. Weapons of violence and warfare are also laid aside or become tools for agricultural work.

24 Perry B. Yoder, *Shalom: The Bible's Word for Salvation, Justice and Peace* (Nappanee, IN: Evangel Publishing House, 1998), 11-13.

25 P. Yoder, *Shalom*, 13-15.

speak falsely.[26] Yoder's discussion includes commentary on shalom's relationship to ancient Israel's law and the development of its political institutions, extending into the first century CE. As these institutions shifted from the time of the judges to the era of kingship with its accompanying structures, and ultimately to Roman imperialism, God's expectation of (political) leaders was constant: it is their duty "to implement substantive justice which leads to shalom."[27]

The word *eirene*, the Greek New Testament's counterpart to shalom, adds another layer of meaning that enlarges shalom's theological meaning. Yoder points out that in Paul's letters, the apostle refers to eirene tou Theou, the peace of God, which Paul uses to interpret the gospel. This new meaning builds on God's interest in justice within social relationships by bringing God's relationship with us into the dynamic. There can only be shalom between people and God, Yoder writes, "because things have been made right between them. The result of Christ's transforming death is not only a transformation of human-divine relationships, but it also transforms affairs between people."[28] Shalom is the site of social transformation where God renews communities.

A Realist Hermeneutical Move

Howard John Loewen has made a study of HPC denominational statements on the theme of peace, in which he observes that their documents cite 98 references from 26 biblical books, with roughly two-thirds of these references coming from the NT.[29] Undoubtedly, the Gospels provide the Christian tradition with resources for developing a "peace theology" based on Jesus' teachings and invitation to people in his time and in our day to become his disciples. However, our reliance on the Gospel accounts does not mean that we have turned our backs on the OT altogether. Most often those who have taken on the challenge of working with the Hebrew Bible have followed the scholars who diverge from Gerhard von Rad's path and the "anti-kingship tradition" of biblical studies. Millard C. Lind's work

---

26 P. Yoder, *Shalom*, 15-16.

27 P. Yoder, *Shalom*, 100.

28 P. Yoder, *Shalom*, 20-21.

29 Howard John Loewen, "An Analysis of the Use of Scripture in the Churches' Documents on Peace," in *The Church's Peace Witness*, ed. Marlin E. Miller and Barbara Nelson Gingerich (Grand Rapids, MI: Eerdmans, 1994), 19.

stands out here: *Yahweh is a Warrior: The Theology of Warfare in Ancient Israel.*[30]

However, there is another course we might follow in relation to peace theology and the Bible. Rather than look backwards from the NT to the OT, we can employ a hermeneutic that looks forward, highlighting how social justice concerns naturally figure in the biblical material. Instead of working within the traditional paradigms of OT biblical theology, we can use this discipline to establish signposts for making thematic and genre connections within the Bible's diversity, and thereby build a bypass of sorts around the traditional "holy way thickets." These signposts are the prophets,[31] wisdom literature,[32] and shalom (this last is the canonical biblical principle at the center of everything).[33]

This is a Christian realist move inspired by my readings of Reinhold Niebuhr and Martin Luther King, Jr. Breaking with some streams of Mennonite scholarship, I am not interested in whether or not God is nonviolent. I am interested in arguing that biblical warfare is an example of human nature at work: self-interest, self-deception, anxiety, and hubris in all their glory. As such, I do not believe that God purposefully wills warfare, because it violates the moral foundation of the universe, which is God's Great Shalom. Violence is never redemptive, even if and when it is effective in confronting evil. The theological meaning we make of violence through our God-given reason, imagination, and memory is where God's redemptive power shines through. Thus, it is the renunciation of violence that is redemptive. I arrive at these conclusions by drawing on the Bible's wisdom literature.

Wisdom's Shalom Theology

In *A Theological Introduction to the Old Testament*, Bruce Birch, Walter Brueggemann, Terence Fretheim, and David Petersen explain that "Old Testament theology" simply refers to interpretive moves that take seriously "the claim of the text that it is speaking about encounter and relationship

---

30 Millard C. Lind, *Yahweh Is a Warrior: The Theology of Warfare in Ancient Israel* (Scottdale, PA: Herald Press, 1980).

31 See Matt. 13:53-58, Mark 6:1-6a, and Luke 4:16-30.

32 Rosemary Radford Ruether, *Sexism and God-talk: Toward a Feminist Theology* (Boston: Beacon Press, 1993), 67-68.

33 Yoder, *Shalom*, 5.

with God."[34] Although the OT is a "collection of polyphonic voices," the authors argue that while this feature is a gift, it also signals the importance of locating the coherence and continuity of Israel's encounter with God as Israel becomes the ethos of the incarnation and the early church. The OT, then, is focused on God's character and activity within the framing context of Israel's story as God's people.[35]

Alongside the historical narratives and law, biblical literature includes the genre of wisdom literature (Proverbs, Job, Ecclesiastes, Ecclesiasticus, and Wisdom of Solomon), which Birch et al. acknowledge is a "broad and imprecise" category. Yet, they argue, there are five characteristics of these books that form what I would call interpretive principles that give wisdom literature its coherence.

First, wisdom literature concerns itself with everyday things like speech, money, friendship, work, sexuality, and land, rather than events such as the Hebrews' exodus from Egypt. Second, in bringing readers' attention to the stuff of life, wisdom literature gives voice to its writers' view that "these mundane matters [are] shot through with ethical significance and ethical outcomes," giving us cause to bring our own experience to theological reflection. Third, "the wisdom teachers want to communicate to the young— those still to be inducted into the lore of the community— its distinctive sense of how life is to be lived well." Fourth, wisdom writers have made careful and studied observations of the world around them that offer a form of systems analysis, to speak anachronistically.[36] Fifth, and most important for SPT, wisdom literature is theological literature (contrary to claims that this literature is insufficiently religious or confessional) by speaking of Yahweh's creative work and intention for the world:

> It is widely recognized that wisdom theology is a 'theology of creation,' that is, a reflection of faith upon the world intended by the creator. It is clear that the creator God intends that the world should be whole, safe, prosperous, peaceable, just, fruitful, and productive, that is, that the world should be marked in every part by shalom. To that end, the creator God has set limits and built into creation rewards and punishments that are evoked and

---

34 Bruce C. Birch, Walter Brueggemann, Terence Fretheim, and David Petersen, *A Theological Introduction to the Old Testament* (Nashville: Abingdon Press, 1999), 17.

35 Birch et al., *Theological Introduction to the Old Testament*, 30.

36 Birch et al., *Theological Introduction to the Old Testament*, 374–76.

> set in motion by wise or foolish actions. But these limits are not self-evident. They must be discerned over a long period of time by the study of many "cases," in order to notice what actions produce trouble. The premise of all such observations and generalizations is that the large matrix of life and well-being is the creation of God. The creator God has willed that all parts of creation are delicately related to one another, and therefore every decision, every act matters to the shape and well-being of the whole.[37]

The wisdom writers offer a global, cosmopolitan rhetoric of biblical faith. They urge us to read these scriptural texts as literature that moves us beyond "clichéd Christianity," favoring an openness that affirms a basic fact: "life in God's world is a way of faith to be celebrated."[38] Their conclusion describes a hermeneutic that encourages us to weave wisdom's insight together with the prophets' oracles of hope and judgment. The wisdom-prophecy tapestry poses an important challenge to readings that advance chosenness-, nation-, and exceptionalist-centered interpretations of the OT.

H. H. Schmid offers further support for this unconventional approach to biblical theology.[39] In the 1970s, Schmid began advocating for reading the OT corpus with a focus on Creation—the beginning of the world and the nature of its order under God's law—rather than a focus on Israel's history as an ethnically defined nation. His approach calls for an emphasis on peace, running contrary to the trend developed and defended by Gerhard von Rad that views warfare, specifically holy warfare, as "a very central and positive element of the entire theology of the Old Testament."[40]

Commentator James Barr argues that Schmid rejects the holy war paradigm of biblical theology because it is based on "a nationally limited understanding of God which is closely connected with the ancient understanding of the world."[41] This means that an ethnocentric quality

---

37 Birch et al., *Theological Introduction to the Old Testament*, 376.

38 Birch et al., *Theological Introduction to the Old Testament*, 377.

39 James Barr, *The Concept of Biblical Theology: An Old Testament Perspective* (Minneapolis: Fortress Press, 1999), 327.

40 Barr, *Concept of Biblical Theology*, 326.

41 Barr, *Concept of Biblical Theology*, 326.

takes hold of biblical interpretation, leading to a view of the cosmos as composed of the chosen and the unchosen. When the world is centered on and ordered around such a particular ethnos, then "the enemies, the foreign peoples [to that ethnos], are basically seen as manifestations of chaos and have to be repelled in the interests of the cosmos."[42] If we rely on this paradigm, then we neglect the witness of a fundamental character of Creation. Schmid writes, "die Bibel geht davon aus, daß der Frieden die eigentliche Bestimmung der Welt ist"[43] ("the Bible proceeds on this basis, that peace is the world's real destiny"). To this Barr adds that understanding peace as the world's destiny becomes a statement about "a basic need of humanity to live in a sound, ordered world."[44] However, this peace is not the Pax Romana or a desperate repression of conflict. It is God's shalom.

Together, the biblical perspectives of Birch, Brueggemann, Fretheim, Petersen, Yoder, and Schmid, and what I read as their theological implications, provide the hermeneutics I am advocating: a way of reading the Bible with a view of the world and human identity that extends beyond a narrow definition of "God's chosen people," one that reads the biblical witness as a sourcebook documenting human beings' navigation of the interplay of violence and nonviolence. When we lay aside a rigid hermeneutics of chosenness—the idea that the Bible is simply the story of Israel—we are able to adopt an intercultural reading of the biblical text which puts cultural differences in relationship with each other, rather than elevating one set of cultural norms above others. Taking a "global" view of the world allows us to pay attention to the biblical message that everything is connected. It is from this organic sense of wholeness that I now turn to a brief outline of SPT's theo-ethical components built on this biblical and theological foundation.

Shalom Political Theology

In aligning with Evans's and Soelle's approaches to political theology that draw attention to the pervasiveness of injustice, SPT can meet urgent demands for justice with an attitude of wisdom. However clear an act of injustice may be, it cannot simply be overcome by human willpower to

---

42 Barr, *Concept of Biblical Theology*, 326.

43 Hans Heinrich Schmid, *Altorientalische Welt in der Alttestamentlichen Theologie*, 6 Aufsätze (Zürich: Theologischer Verlag, 1974), 116.

44 Barr, *Concept of Biblical Theology*, 327.

defy sin, evil, and oppression. "If we just mobilize enough volunteers." "If we can just get enough signatures on our petition." "If we can just prove they are behind this outrage." "What they're doing is just wrong!" Self-righteous anger alone is not enough to solve our problems. Moreover, when we begin with an interest in shalom, we look at the world through the lenses of sin and grace. To seek God's shalom for the world involves paying attention to how sin (unbelief, rebellion, inordinate self-love, self-deception) decimates relationships and how grace (repentance, humility, renewed trust, forgiveness) preserves them. Only when we can see both types of power at work in the world will we be ready to conceptualize what it means to welcome God's shalom into our lives and into that world.

SPT integrates a cluster of theo-ethical principles that draw on three theo-ethicists: theological anthropology informed by Christian realist Reinhold Niebuhr, nonviolence informed by personalist Martin Luther King, Jr., and Doris Janzen Longacre's feminist reconstruction of nonconformity. Because I am committed to interpreting and applying SPT in real, live communities, SPT includes three practices that make integrating the three principles possible: transparency in naming the influential members in our communities, nonviolent communication, and the discipline of circle process.

Realistic Theological Anthropology

One of Niebuhr's contributions to 20th-century Christian thought is an insistence that "sin" is a necessary, not dirty, word in our theological vocabulary. Through his pastoral work, activism, and academic work, Niebuhr came to the conclusion that American liberal theology had led Christians down the wrong path. By sentimentalizing Jesus' message "beyond all recognition," liberal Christianity was dismissing the biblical foundations of Christian faith, replacing them with middle-class idealism and moralizing. Niebuhr took an alternative path "theologically to the right and politically to the left of modern liberal Protestantism," and urged others to join him in taking an existentialist view of the Bible's ideas and insights about human beings.[45]

In the preface to a 1964 edition of *The Nature and Destiny of Man*, Niebuhr explains his basic thesis that Western culture has emphasized

---

45 Reinhold Niebuhr, "Dr. Niebuhr's Position," *The Christian Century* 50 (1933): 91-92, quoted in Gary J. Dorrien, *Idealism, Realism, and Modernity: 1900-1950* (Louisville: Westminster John Knox Press, 2003), 451.

two ideas—individuality and meaningful history—that are actually rooted in the Hebraic biblical tradition. In tracing "the growth, corruption, and purification of these two concepts," he hopes his two volumes might "create a better understanding between the historic roots and the several disciplines of our modern culture which were concerned with the human situation."[46] The biblical roots to which Niebuhr brought new attention involve the enduring paradox of human beings, the fact that we carry in us God's image while also being finite creatures. This paradox, held dialectically, is the foundation of Niebuhr's theological anthropology.

A second dialectic that grounds this anthropology and Niebuhr's theology overall is a vertical dialectic of transcendence and relatedness. Langdon Gilkey identifies a three-fold use of transcendence in Niebuhr's theology: transcendence as anchored in God beyond our immediate reality; as the ground of reality, meaning, judgment, and hope; and as self-transcendence, our capacity to rise above self-interest and relate to God. "Despite the fact that transcendence as Niebuhr sees it is not an aspect of the human psyche or of cultural history, this is a transcendence continually related to the world—related, that is, not only to individual persons, but even more to society, culture, and history."[47]

"God, grant me the serenity to accept the things I cannot change, the courage to change the things I can, and the wisdom to know the difference": this prayer attributed to Niebuhr is a microcosm of his theological anthropology. There is an appeal to God, who transcends and judges human history and culture; there is hope that, through our relationship with God, we may discern how self-interest and self-deception distort the *imago Dei*, leading us to think we can change anything we think should be changed; and there is reassurance that our creaturely freedom can also be a source of inspiration to combat injustice.

Nonviolence and Beloved Community

Martin Luther King, Jr. did not begin his career as an activist but as a Baptist preacher. Finding himself leading a movement for civil rights came as a surprise to the young King, who had become a sought-after orator and hoped to eventually occupy an academic chair. As the movement took off, he became aware that he needed to apply his theological education

---

46 Reinhold Niebuhr, *The Nature and Destiny of Man: A Christian Interpretation* (New York: Charles Scribner's Sons, 1964), vii.

47 Langdon Gilkey, *On Niebuhr: A Theological Study* (Chicago: Univ. of Chicago Press, 2001), 17, emphasis Gilkey's.

to tasks that involved more than sermon writing and pastoral care. As he applied religious belief to moral and political action, he was not simply drawing from the wells of his graduate school experience; he was also integrating theo-ethical lessons learned in childhood into what would become a full-scale system of theology. King scholar and personalist Rufus Burrow, Jr. has coined this system "Afrikan American Personalism," linking King's intellectual training with the Boston school of personalism and his "homespun" personalism that was integral to his view of God, human beings, love, and justice.[48] Burrow names five personalist ideas that animate King's theology and ethics, specifically his belief in nonviolence and his vision of the beloved community: reality is personal; reality is social; "persons" are of the highest intrinsic value; the universe is based on an objective moral order; and social injustice requires our protest as we establish a community of love.[49]

The goal of King's activism was the recognition of the human worth and dignity of all peoples and their inclusion in the "world house." Nonviolence was not merely a tactic for him; it indicated the kind of relationship he wanted black people to have with their neighbors, whether white, black, or brown. In 1966 King wrote about these dynamics in an essay on nonviolence, in the face of competing calls from other activists for violence and self-defense: "The American racial revolution has been a revolution to 'get in' rather than to overthrow. We want a share in the American economy, the housing market, the educational system, and the social opportunities. This goal itself indicates that a social change in America must be nonviolent."[50]

This conviction is directly connected to King's characterization of nonviolence as a way of life that does not seek to humiliate one's opponent but to bring both self and opponent to the same side, the side of God's justice; these are the politics of shalom. With his optimism, held in dialectical tension with Niebuhrian realism about the morality of groups within society, King argued that an outcome of nonviolence is the beloved

---

48 Burrow uses the Black Consciousness spelling of Afrika, which, he writes, is a prevalent and preferred spelling on the continent and in the diaspora. Rufus Burrow, Jr., *God and Human Dignity: The Personalism, Theology, and Ethics of Martin Luther King Jr.* (Notre Dame: Univ. of Notre Dame Press, 2006), 2.

49 Burrow, *God and Human Dignity*, 86.

50 Martin Luther King, Jr., "Nonviolence: The Only Road to Freedom," in *A Testament of Hope: The Essential Writings and Speeches of Martin Luther King Jr.*, ed. James Melvin Washington (San Francisco: HarperSanFrancisco, 1991), 58.

community, a reality created cooperatively by God and human beings, a reality that appears in our midst here and in our speaking prophetic words of judgment, and in our daily decisions to suffer rather than retaliate, and to live as mystics who notice how God is at work in the world.[51]

Feminist Reconstruction of Nonconformity

Reconstruction is an approach to theology's constructive task that identifies the need to take things apart (deconstruct) and then put them back together in a process that may use different materials, design, and techniques. One model for such reconstruction has been generated by the Workgroup on Constructive Theology, a collective that has authored a number of theology texts, including *Reconstructing Christian Theology*.[52] Within theology's new discursive context, Workgroup members advocate for analyzing Christian doctrine with "the goal of shaping a revisioned Christian communal praxis," the word "communal" signaling the variety of communities now involved in the production of theology.[53]

One of the multiple junctures where reconstructive work happens is the place where we decide to reformulate what a doctrine symbolizes rather than rejecting it outright. This process involves naming the ways traditional doctrinal formulation has contributed to the current crisis, resulting in Christian theology's anemic response to pressing social issues and problems. A second juncture is reclaiming theologians' work of speaking directly to particular communities and society as a whole, sharing new insights that emerge from the reconstructive process. Rebecca Chopp and Mark Taylor note that "alternative modes of address, perhaps employing the poetic or mixing words and images in novel ways, may be extremely important today for reconstructing an engagement of theologians with artists and activists, who are especially needed for social and ecclesial transformation."[54]

In this vein, Doris Janzen Longacre, starting with a cookbook, has reconstructed the Anabaptist/Mennonite doctrine of nonconformity (based on Romans 12:2, 1 John 2:15-16, and 1 Peter 2:11). Describing

---

51 See various sermons and addresses in *The Papers of Martin Luther King Jr.*, vol. 4, ed. Clayborne Carson et al. (Berkeley: Univ. of California Press, 2000). See Burrow, *God and Human Dignity*, 169.

52 Rebecca S. Chopp and Mark Lewis Taylor, eds., *Reconstructing Christian Theology* (Minneapolis: Fortress Press, 1994).

53 Chopp and Taylor, *Reconstructing Christian Theology*, 12.

54 Chopp and Taylor, "Introduction," in *Reconstructing Christian Theology*, 20.

Mennonites as good cooks who also care about the world's hungry in the preface to *More-with-Less*, Longacre deftly recasts this cultural heritage in spiritual terms: "We are looking for ways to live more simply and joyfully, ways that grow out of our tradition but take their shape from living faith and the demands of our hungry world."[55] Part 1 of *Living More with Less* gives Longacre's biblical, theological, and ethical foundations for putting this new consciousness about the world into action. She outlines five principles or standards to guide theological reflection: (1) do justice, (2) learn from the world community, (3) cherish the natural order, (4) nurture people, (5) nonconform freely.[56] While these principles may seem obvious, the next question she addresses adds considerable complexity: How might these theological norms become concrete action?

With the fifth standard, Longacre freed a valuable biblical idea that had, by the 1950s and '60s, become ideologically and ethically entrenched as church leaders sought to keep "worldliness" out of their congregations and communities. From her vantage point, Longacre saw that the rigidity of not conforming to the world had lost both its prophetic edge and its possibility of symbolizing freedom, joy, and transformation. Seeking to recapture the apostle Paul's radical message, she proposed a new, reconstructed approach to nonconformity marked by individual and communal choices to free ourselves from patterns of overconsumption and the imperialist mentality that equates affluence with wisdom.

While Longacre never identified herself or her work as explicitly feminist, she was deeply committed to viewing the world as one gigantic ecosystem and did not shy away from naming the evils of imperial exploitation from her social location as a woman. This fits with a primary philosophical tenet of feminist theory and theology: patriarchy creates and maintains an ontological hierarchy to keep a small number of (male) people in control by using mechanisms of exploitation and oppression, particularly by dominating female bodies, symbols, and concepts, including the planet. Longacre's reconstruction of nonconformity as a practice of Christian freedom challenges North American hubris, raises awareness about the dehumanizing features of our cultures, and makes these issues

---

55 Doris Janzen Longacre, *More-with-Less Cookbook* (Scottdale, PA: Herald Press, 1998), 13.

56 Doris Janzen Longacre, *Living More with Less* (Scottdale, PA: Herald Press, 1980), 21ff. While Longacre describes these "life standards" as her alternative way of speaking about "lifestyle," she notes that "standard is a word that fits a way of life governed by more than fleeting taste. It is permanent and firm without being as tight as 'rules'" (16).

theo-ethical problems. Following the path of her analysis in combination with Niebuhr and King, I see a way forward to a theologically rich understanding of Christian discipleship invested in all people's wellbeing.

Three Practices of Shalom Political Theology

In *Artists, Citizens, Philosophers: Seeking the Peace of the City—An Anabaptist Theology of Culture*, Duane Friesen describes the importance of "focal practices," the ontological commitments, lifestyle choices, and behaviors that express a community's vision of the common good, for well-grounded moral formation.[57] Friesen's discussion of rituals of moral formation, process practices, pastoral care, and practices of service has drawn my attention to how my own moral formation and primary socialization in Mennonite community taught me more about avoiding conflict under the guise of "peacemaking" than about pursuing shalom. What draws me to Niebuhr, King, and Longacre is how their ideas provide tools to develop a multivalent outward/inward awareness of my life as a Christian, the group dynamics of my congregation, the institutional and interpersonal challenges of my workplace, and an understanding of what those things have to do with the rest of the world. Thus, if SPT is to be a meaningful alternative to the pacifism of the Messianic community, I believe it must include formative shalom practices so that Mennonite communities are no longer easy prey to the criticism that we are more ready to help our global neighbors solve their conflicts than we are to face our own. I will now briefly summarize three ways I have been practicing SPT.[58]

First is naming the influential members of my faith community as such. As a corrective to the over-zealousness of bishops, Anabaptist interpretations of "the priesthood of all believers" can turn this principle into a false egalitarianism. Using the theo-ethics of SPT, I have seen how integrity takes root when groups come to terms with the fact that some people's opinions count more than others. The Quaker tradition of recognizing "weighty Friends" as those who have spiritual maturity and theological

---

57 Duane Friesen, *Artists, Citizens, Philosophers: Seeking the Peace of the City—An Anabaptist Theology of Culture* (Scottdale, PA: Herald Press, 2005), 139ff.

58 I am at work on a book-length project that elaborates on these practices, relating their pragmatic wisdom to wisdom literature's appropriations of social justice codes, providing a pattern for how to integrate and theologize practices that come to us without a particular confessional or religious orientation, which is true for two of these practices. These practices can be particularly useful in conflicts centered on sexual violence, a moral and social problem that some types of peace theology inexcusably exacerbate.

insight that gives their opinions more authority in times of conflict or discernment is one that Mennonite peace theologies can learn from. Such naming creates a climate of honesty about how power dynamics shape our interactions with each other, making it possible to speak more truthfully about the internal politics of being church.

Second is nonviolent communication (NVC), a communication process developed by clinical psychologist Marshall B. Rosenberg that cultivates empathy and compassion as requisites for personal and communal well-being.[59] By practicing NVC's pattern of observing without judgment, identifying emotions and needs in light of observation, and making requests (not demands) based on emotions and needs, I have realized how much my communal formation taught me to communicate passive-aggressively with inadequate vocabulary for communication that nurtures empathic connection and assertiveness. When we mistake peace theo-ethics for conflict avoidance, we sacrifice our well-being, pacifying ourselves with self-righteousness instead of enacting shalom. Jesus does not ask us to love our neighbors more or instead of ourselves, he urges us to love our neighbors and ourselves. NVC is one concrete way to explore how a commitment to nonviolence can manifest the double-love command (Matt. 22:34-40, Mark 12:28-34, Luke 10:25-28).

Third is circle process, a practice of creating a social container for all voices to be heard and valued in what M. Scott Peck calls "real community."[60] This practice intersects with NVC, and together they are powerful tools for addressing painful topics and celebrating what is good in the world. There are many ways and reasons to form circles; diversity circles and restorative justice circles are well-known examples. My circle practice is based on a model called PeerSpirit Circling and the Circle Way.[61] Through this practice in the classroom, in congregational life, and even at the extended family dinner table, I have been astounded at what happens when we begin to rely on everyone to carry and shape the conversation, instead of the usual suspects. Breaking with cultural norms that make in-

---

[59] Marshall B. Rosenberg, *Nonviolent Communication: A Language of Life*, 3rd ed. (Encinitas, CA: PuddleDancer Press, 2015).

[60] Christina Baldwin and Ann Linnea, *The Circle Way: A Leader in Every Chair* (San Francisco: Berrett-Koehler Publishers, 2010), 12. M. Scott Peck, *The Different Drum: Community Making and Peace* (New York: Touchstone, 1998), 59.

[61] Along with Baldwin and Linnea, The Circle Way, websites for PeerSpirit (http://peerspirit.com/) and Calling the Circle (http://callingthecircle.org/) provide introductions to PeerSpirit Circling.

terruption inevitable and silence uncomfortable, circle process has given me a way to explore SPT as a theo-ethic of nonconformity and spiritual renewal. I have seen shalom happen when people ask for what they need from the circle, and I have heard people bear witness to how sharing in another's vulnerability taught them something new about what it means to be a Christian.

Conclusion

SPT grounds a commitment to peace, justice, nonviolence, and nonconformity in a theological anthropology that takes sin and power dynamics seriously. My hope is that SPT also grounds socially responsible political engagement, challenging our often employed but simplistic biblical hermeneutics that identify the Christian call to pacifism with Jesus' words commanding us to love our enemies. This approach all too often and all too easily fails to avoid ideological pitfalls with hubris masquerading as righteousness. Peace theology and ethics employing a realistic view of human nature lead to moral formation that curbs our tendencies toward making sharp binary distinctions. For example, the statement of the National Council of Churches of Christ in the USA that "war is contrary to the will of God" was not originally a pacifistic statement. However, some Christians read it pacifistically, leading to an interpretation that makes a pacifistic view of Christian faith theologically normative rather than allowing for a variety of faithful understandings. Once this kind of claim becomes normative, Christians begin to advocate for public policies to outlaw war. When this happens, we draw a divide between those who are moral and those who are immoral; in the cosmic barnyard, pacifists are the sheep and warmongers are the goats. This was one of Niebuhr's chief reasons for leaving the Christian pacifist position and developing a realistic view of theological anthropology, which SPT emphasizes.

When peace theology sheds the language of pacifism and takes up the language of nonviolence in the tradition of King, it also reorients itself to a metaphysics that envisions shalom. This turn underscores both the agency we have as free persons and the fragility of this freedom in a society with the power to structure our lives in ways that distort our dignity and confine our choices.

Generations of contemporary Mennonites across subcultures learned that peacemaking meant avoiding conflict, objecting to war as a matter of conscience, and "loving our enemies," but we need something more if we are going to proclaim a gospel that renounces violence. Looking back, we can see that if we reduce peace theology to avoiding conflict, then it will only ever be a theo-ethics of privilege. And if we reduce it to an orientation of personal obedience to communal norms, then it will only ever be a peculiar form of discipleship. If, however, we enact peace theology as a theo-ethics seeking shalom as a way of imagining God's politics, then our witness becomes a form of social engagement with the world that hopes for personal and communal transformation. Shalom is a way of invoking the power of life's goodness despite the suffering, exploitation, violence, and alienation that remind us that evil is as powerful as ever. Shalom is invested in the quality of our living and loving. Shalom paints vivid pictures of opposites embracing—unlikely allies laughing with abandon as they break bread together, wolves and lambs enjoying the shade of the same tree, an unshakeable sense that we belong.

Afterword

As I mention in my 2016 essay that has been included in this edition, I used to have a stack of the *Panorama* in my office, but my stash has been depleted. I am thus grateful that the volume you are reading is available in this updated edition. Your role, as a reader, is crucial in ensuring that the ideas found here continue to benefit new generations of Mennonites and enrich old and new conversations within the global Mennonite community. In other words, the *Panorama*'s evangelical task is not done.

In the intervening years since I wrote the essay, the world has continued to be a dynamic place, and the convictions I laid out in my essay have only deepened. What have also deepened are the polarizations and chasms in every sphere of life: the rich get richer and the poor poorer, the Right and the Left are further apart around the world, perceived moral rights and wrongs clash in school board meetings and public library stacks across both Canada and the United States. Where I live, what you think about guns, artificial intelligence, bathrooms, fossil fuels, vaccinations, and social media are all potential sites not merely of difference but also of hot, entrenched conflict. Standing in the gaps and hot spots takes practice, endurance, and courage because we will keep making mistakes, including making idols of the early Anabaptists and "peace" itself.

In the intervening years since I contributed my ideas to Mennonite peace theology, I have also added books to my shelves about spiritual activism, conflict transformation, wholeheartedness, and healing societal wounds. These sit beside my collection of children's books. Some tell tender stories about mindfulness, feelings, and emotional self-regulation. Others teach people of all ages new ways to hear our ancient, meaning-making stories. Still others offer glimpses into times, places, and communities that the Holy Spirit is calling us to remember so we can retell old stories. I believe that our concern for sound theological teaching, ethics, and biblical interpretation must be expanded to include a concern for our emotions and passions, the things that move us to keep faith, hope, and love alive and share God's vision of a peaceable kindom with others.

In the intervening years since I committed myself to stewarding our tradition of peace theology, our planet's climate crisis has intensified. The call to steward Earth's resources, along with a theological tradition, has focused my sense of vocation. Wherever you may find yourself in this panoramic conversation, I want you to use the ideas you find here to draw you into the "housework" our species has set before us, because the crisis we face in the physical environment is paralleled in the way we treat ourselves and each other. The five life standards of Doris Janzen Longacre's *Living More with Less* inspire me, and I hope you, to use peace theology as a pathway that leads us to the kind of maturity our world demands of Christian people.

First, any community that seeks to do justice (i.e., to live by both reason and compassion) will have a need for accountants, artists, and everyone in between. How do your commitments to nonviolence weave together differing disciplines, professions, personalities, and abilities? Second, as global citizens who learn from the world community, we seek counsel from neighborhoods near and far so that we are truthful about the challenges of not just underdevelopment but overdevelopment, too. How do your ethics dance with socioeconomic class? Third, we face a leadership challenge: How do we lead our congregations, institutions, organizations, communities, and families in ways that nurture people by working against exploitation and in harmony with the planet? Fourth, we must face the ongoing temptation to reshape the environment to fit the way we want to live rather than consciously choosing to cherish the natural order and our place within it. Can peace theology inspire us to turn toward cooperation and harmony with nature? Finally, mature Christians embrace the gifts of nonconforming freely. There are many dynamics at work in the world that distract us from loving God and embracing the power God gives us to feel, learn, grow, change, forgive, repair, and follow Jesus everywhere he goes. Where is the Prince of Peace inviting you to go?

Malinda Elizabeth Berry
Associate Professor of Theology and Ethics
Anabaptist Mennonite Biblical Seminary
Elkhart, Indiana

Bibliography

Barrett, Lois. "A critique of 'Political Nonviolence.'" Paper presented at the joint meeting of the MCC Peace Committee and Ecumenical Peace Theology Working Group, 3-4 November 1989, Elkhart, Indiana.

Burkholder, J. Lawrence. *The Problem of Social Responsibility from the Perspective of the Mennonite Church.* Elkhart, IN: Institute of Mennonite Studies, 1989. [Reprinted in J. Lawrence Burkholder, *Mennonite Ethics: From Isolation to Engagement*, edited by Lauren Friesen. Victoria, BC: Friesen Press, 2018.]

Burkholder, J. R. "Can We Make Sense out of Mennonite Peace Theology?" Working draft presented at the joint meeting of the MCC Peace Committee and Ecumenical Peace Theology Working Group, 3-4 November 1989, Elkhart, Indiana; reprinted in the present volume.

Burkholder, J. R. "Response to Koontz and Redekop." Peace Theology Colloquium IV, 20-23 June 1985, Elkhart, Indiana.

Detweiler, Richard C. *Mennonite Statements on Peace, 1915-1966: A Historical and Theological Review of Anabaptist-Mennonite Concepts of Peace Witness and Church-State Relations.* Scottdale, PA: Herald Press, 1968.

Driedger, Leo. *Mennonites in Winnipeg.* Winnipeg: Kindred Press, 1990.

Fowler, James W. "Black Theologies of Liberation: A Structural-Developmental Analysis." In *The Challenge of Liberation Theology: A First World Response*, edited by Brian Mahan and L. Dale Richesin, 69-90. Maryknoll, NY: Orbis Books, 1981.

Friesen, Duane K. *Christian Peacemaking and International Conflict: A Realist Pacifist Perspective.* Scottdale, PA: Herald Press, 1986.

Friesen, Duane. *Mennonite Witness on Peace and Social Concerns: 1900-1980.* Akron, PA: Mennonite Central Committee, 1982.

Goerz, H. "The Cultural Life among the Mennonites of Russia." *Mennonite Life* 24 (July 1969): 99-100.

Grimsrud, Ted. "Response to Ted Koontz's Paper: Mennonites and the State." Peace Theology Colloquium IV, 20-23 June 1985, Elkhart, Indiana.

Harder, Leland, ed. *The Sources of Swiss Anabaptism: The Grebel Letters and Related Documents.* Scottdale, PA: Herald Press, 1985.

Hershberger, Guy Franklin. *The Mennonite Church in the Second World War.* Scottdale, PA: Mennonite Publishing House, 1951.

Hershberger, Guy Franklin. "Nonviolence." In *The Mennonite Encyclopedia.* Vol. 3. Scottdale, PA: Mennonite Publishing House, 1957.

Hershberger, Guy Franklin. "Our Citizenship Is in Heaven." In *Kingdom, Cross, and Community: Essays on Mennonite Themes in Honor of Guy F. Hershberger,* edited by John Richard Burkholder and Calvin Redekop, 273-85. Scottdale, PA: Herald Press, 1976.

Hershberger, Guy Franklin. *War, Peace and Nonresistance.* Scottdale, PA: Herald Press, 1944 (1953, 1969).

Hershberger, Guy Franklin. *The Way of the Cross in Human Relations.* Scottdale, PA: Herald Press, 1958.

Juhnke, James C. *Dialogue with a Heritage.* North Newton, KS: Bethel College, 1987.

Juhnke, James C. "Mennonite History and Self-understanding: North American Mennonitism as a Bipolar Mosaic." In *Mennonite Identity: Historical and Contemporary Perspectives,* edited by Calvin Wall Redekop and Samuel J. Steiner, 83-100. Lanaham, MD: University Press of America, 1988.

Juhnke, James C. *Vision, Doctrine, War.* Scottdale, PA: Herald Press, 1989.

Kaufman, E. G. *The Development of the Missionary and Philanthropic Interests among the Mennonites of North America.* Berne, IN: Berne Book Concern, 1931.

Kaufman, E. G. *Our Mission as a Church of Christ.* Newton, KS: Faith and Life Press, 1944.

Kaufman, Gordon D. *Nonresistance and Responsibility.* Newton, KS: Faith and Life Press, 1979.

Kaufman, Gordon D. "The Significance of Art." *Mennonite Life* 20 (January 1965): 5-7.

Klassen, N. J. "Mennonite Intelligentsia in Russia." *Mennonite Life* 24 (April 1969): 51-60.

Klippenstein, Lawrence. "Mennonite Pacifism and State Service in Russia." PhD diss., University of Minnesota, 1984.

Koontz, Gayle Gerber, and Perry Yoder. "Issues and Questions Raised during the IMS-MCC Peace Colloquium." In *Essays on Peace Theology and Witness*, edited by Willard H. Swartley, 210-12. Elkhart, IN: Institute of Mennonite Studies, 1985.

Koontz, Ted. "Mennonites and the State: Preliminary Reflections." In *Essays on Peace Theology and Witness*, edited by Willard H. Swartley, 35-60. Elkhart, IN: Institute of Mennonite Studies, 1988.

Krehbiel, H. P. *A Trip through Europe: A Plea for the Abolition of War*. Newton, KS: Herald Publishing, 1926.

Krehbiel, H. P. *War, Peace, Amity*. Newton, KS: Herald Publishing, 1937.

Lapp, John A. *The Mennonite Church in India*. Scottdale, PA: Herald Press, 1972.

Lichdi, Dieter Goetz. *Mennonite World Handbook*. Carol Stream, IL: Mennonite World Conference, 1990.

Míguez Bonino, José. *La fe en busca de eficacia*. Salamanca, Spain: Ediciones Sigueme, 1977.

Míguez Bonino, José. "On Discipleship, Justice and Power." In *Freedom and Discipleship*, edited Daniel S. Schipani, 131-38. Maryknoll, NY: Orbis Books, 1989.

Neufeld, Mark. "Critical Theory and Christian Service: Knowledge and Action in Situations of Conflict." *Conrad Grebel Review* 6, no. 3 (1988): 249-62.

Niebuhr, H. Richard. *Christ and Culture*. New York: Harper & Row, 1951.

Pickering, Jerry V. "Medieval Origins of European Folk Dramas." Paper presented at the Association for Theater in Higher Education Conference, 9 August 1988, Chicago.

Pixley, George V. "Response from a Baptist Biblical Scholar." In *Freedom and Discipleship*, edited by Daniel S. Schipani, 139-46. Maryknoll, NY: Orbis Books, 1989.

Ramsey, Paul. *Basic Christian Ethics*. New York: Scribners, 1950.

Redekop, John H. "Mennonites and Politics in Canada and the United States." *Journal of Mennonite Studies* 1 (1983): 79-105.

Redekop, John H. "The State and the Free Church." In *Kingdom, Cross, and Community: Essays on Mennonite Themes in Honor of Guy F. Hershberger*, edited by John Richard Burkholder and Calvin Redekop, 179-95. Scottdale, PA: Herald Press, 1976.

Richert, P. H. *A Brief Catechism on Difficult Scripture Passages and Involved Questions on the Use of the Sword*. Newton, KS: [Western District Peace Committee], 1942.

Rutenber, Culbert. *The Dagger and the Cross*. New York: Fellowship, 1950.

Sawatzky, Rodney J. "Domesticated Sectarianism: Mennonites in the U.S. and Canada." *Canadian Journal of Sociology* 3, no. 2 (1978): 233-44.

Schlabach, Theron F. *Peace, Faith, Nation*. Scottdale, PA: Herald Press, 1988.

Schlabach, Theron F. "To Focus a Mennonite Vision." In *Kingdom, Cross, and Community: Essays on Mennonite Themes in Honor of Guy F. Hershberger*, edited by John Richard Burkholder and Calvin Redekop, 15-50. Scottdale, PA: Herald Press, 1976.

Schmidt, Kim. "The North Newton WILPF: Educating for Peace." *Mennonite Life* 40 (December 1985): 8-13.

Segundo, Juan Luis. *The Liberation of Theology*. Maryknoll, NY: Orbis Books, 1975.

Sider, Ronald J. *Christ and Violence*. Scottdale, PA: Herald Press, 1979.

Sider, Ronald J. *Completely Pro-life: Building a Consistent Stance*. Downers Grove, IL: InterVarsity Press, 1987.

Sider, Ronald J. *Non-violence: The Invincible Weapon?* Dallas: Word Publishing, 1989.

Sider, Ronald J. *Rich Christians in an Age of Hunger: A Biblical Study*. Downers Grove, IL: InterVarsity Press, 1977.

Snyder, C. Arnold. "The Relevance of Anabaptist Nonviolence for Nicaragua Today." In *Freedom and Discipleship*, edited by Daniel S. Schipani, 112-27. Maryknoll, NY: Orbis Books, 1989; reprinted from *The Conrad Grebel Review* 2, no. 2 (Spring 1984): 123-37.

Toews, John B. *A History of the Mennonite Brethren Church*. Hillsboro, KS: Mennonite Brethren Publishing House, 1975.

Toews, Paul. "The Long Weekend or the Short Week: Mennonite Peace Theology, 1925-1944." *Mennonite Quarterly Review* 60, no. 1 (January 1986): 38-57.

Weaver, J. Denny. *Becoming Anabaptist: The Origin and Significance of Sixteenth-Century Anabaptism*. Scottdale, PA: Herald Press, 1987.

Wedel, C. H. *Meditationen zu den Fragen und Antworten unseres Katechismus.* Newton, KS: Herold Druck, 1911.

Wedel, C. H. *Sketches from Church History for Mennonite Schools.* Translated by Gustav Haury. Newton, KS: Herald Publishing, 1924.

Wedel, D. C. "Contributions of David Goerz." *Mennonite Life* 7 (October 1952): 170.

Wedel, P. J. *The Story of Bethel College.* North Newton, KS: Bethel College, 1954.

Welty, B. F. "Notes from the History of Church Music in America." *Bethel College Monthly* 9 (May 1904): 18.

Wink, Walter. *Violence and Nonviolence in South Africa: Jesus' Third Way.* Philadelphia, PA: New Society Publishers, 1987.

Yoder, John Howard. *The Christian Witness to the State.* Newton, KS: Faith and Life Press, 1964.

Yoder, John Howard. *Nevertheless: The Varieties of Religious Pacifism.* Scottdale, PA: Herald Press, 1971 [1992].

Yoder, John Howard. "Peace without Eschatology." A *Concern* reprint. Scottdale, PA: Herald Press, 1959.

Yoder, John Howard. *The Politics of Jesus.* Grand Rapids: Eerdmans, 1972 [1994].

Yoder, John Howard. *The Priestly Kingdom: Social Ethics as Gospel.* Notre Dame, IN: University of Notre Dame Press, 1984.

Yoder, Perry B. *Shalom: The Bible's Word for Salvation, Justice, and Peace.* Newton, KS: Faith and Life Press, 1987.

Contributors

Editor's note: The following bibliographic information is from the 1991 edition.

Lois Barrett is co-pastor of Mennonite Church of the Servant, Wichita, Kansas, and a PhD candidate in historical theology at The Union Institute, Cincinnati, Ohio. She is the author of five books, including *Doing What Is Right: What the Bible Says about Covenant and Justice.*

John Richard Burkholder is chairperson of the Ecumenical Peace Theology Working Group sponsored by MCC Peace Office. He formerly taught at Goshen College, Goshen, Indiana, and at Associated Mennonite Biblical Seminaries, Elkhart, Indiana, primarily in the fields of ethics, theology, and peace studies.

Lauren Friesen is professor of drama at Goshen College, Goshen, Indiana, and author of numerous plays, including "King David," "House of God," and "Love of John," and a collection of poetry, "Prairie Songs."

Barbara Nelson Gingerich lives in Goshen, Indiana, and is a graduate student in theology at the University of Chicago divinity school. Her dissertation research is on indefinite hold; she currently devotes most of her energies to the care of sons Jonathan (3) and Daniel (1).

Helmut Harder was for many years professor of theology at Canadian Mennonite Bible College, Winnipeg, Manitoba. He is now General Secretary of the Conference of Mennonites in Canada. He also chairs the Peace Committee of Mennonite Central Committee and is co-chair of the GC/MC Confession of Faith Committee. As a member of the International Mennonite Peace Committee of the Mennonite World Conference, he wrote *The Biblical Way of Peace.*

John H. Redekop is professor of political science at Wilfrid Laurier University, Waterloo, Ontario.

Daniel Schipani is professor of Christian education and personality at Associated Mennonite Biblical Seminaries, Elkhart, Indiana. He has written or edited twelve books, in Spanish and English, including *Freedom and Discipleship: Liberation Theology in Anabaptist Perspective.* His ecumenical involvements include membership in the Fraternidad Teológica Latinoamericana, and he lectures in several Hispanic ministries programs in the United States and Latin America.

David Schroeder is professor of Bible at Canadian Mennonite Bible College, Winnipeg, Manitoba.

Arnold Snyder is associate professor of history and peace and conflict studies at Conrad Grebel College, Waterloo, Ontario. He also serves as editor of *The Conrad Grebel Review*.

Robert J. Suderman is a fraternal worker with the Commission on Overseas Ministries of the General Conference Mennonite Church, currently serving in Bogotá, Colombia. He is director and professor at the Mennonite Biblical Seminary of Colombia and director of the Latin American Center for Anabaptist Resources (CLARA). He is also a PhD candidate in New Testament studies at Toronto School of Theology.

www.ingramcontent.com/pod-product-compliance
Lightning Source LLC
Chambersburg PA
CBHW071457150426
43191CB00008B/1377